Twayne's United States Authors Series

Sylvia E. Bowman, *Editor*

INDIANA UNIVERSITY

Henry Blake Fuller

HENRY BLAKE FULLER

By JOHN PILKINGTON, JR.

University of Mississippi

 175

Twayne Publishers, Inc.   : :   New York

HENRY BLAKE FULLER
by
JOHN PILKINGTON, JR.

When Henry Blake Fuller died in 1929, Hamlin Garland, his closest friend for more than thirty-five years, rightly predicted that "Henry B." would soon become a legend in Chicago. If today "Henry B." does not rank as a major writer, he is still remembered in the Windy City by the "cliff-dwellers," and his contribution to American letters cannot be ignored by any literary historian of the 1890's.

In 1879, at the age of twenty-three, Fuller left the raw, ugly, booming metropolis of Chicago, which he already detested, to make the pilgrimage to Italy which Longfellow, Hawthorne, Lowell, Norton, Howells, James, and many other American artists had made long before him. When Fuller returned, a year later, he was convinced that he ought to live in Chicago and write about it in fiction, but he could not put aside his longing for the postroads of Tuscany.

The tension created by the opposing forces of Italy and Chicago weighed heavily upon a personality that could be, by turns, charming or perverse, brilliant or moody, gregarious or eccentric. Yet out of this conflict, which Fuller upon occasion restated for himself as the opposition between Howells and James or between realism and idealism, arose his finest work, *The Chevalier of Pensieri-Vani, The Chatelaine of La Trinité, The Cliff-Dwellers,* and *With the Procession.*

The author of this book, the first extended study of Fuller to be published, has unravelled the sources of Fuller's astonishing brilliance in the 1890's and the reasons for the long and less successful aftermath. The objective of this book has not been to "revive" Fuller, but to examine and interpret the life and writings of an extraordinary man who occupies a very respectable position in the history of American literature.

Preface

Whatever else may be said about Henry Blake Fuller, his life and writings are unique because of the degree to which they were shaped by Chicago and Italy. In 1879, at the age of twenty-three, Fuller left the raw, ugly, but booming metropolis of Chicago to make the pilgrimage to Italy, which had been made long before him by Henry Wadsworth Longfellow, Nathaniel Hawthorne, James Russell Lowell, Charles Eliot Norton, William Dean Howells, and many other Americans. When Fuller returned, a year later, the ideas and patterns of thought which determined his career and provided substance for his books had been firmly established. Henceforth, for much of his life, his residence would be in Chicago but his heart would long for the postroads of Tuscany. The raw force, the energy, the activity of Chicago which Fuller could, upon occasion, respect and even admire, clashed with the charm, the beauty, the art of Italy. Had either of these two places been absent from Fuller's experience, there would have been no need for this book to have been written.

Time, as well as place, favored Fuller. Had he appeared a decade earlier, his criticism of Chicago and his admiration for Italy would have had little impact upon Eastern and Midwestern readers. Fuller was extremely fortunate that his own maturity coincided not only with the phenomenal growth of Chicago but also with the first stirrings of esthetic consciousness in the city. Chicago was ready, in the early part of the 1890's, to identify, acknowledge, and applaud its own native-born literary genius; and, when Fuller seemed to have been "discovered" by the recognized guardians of culture in the East, his reputation in Chicago was established beyond question.

Had Fuller, on the other hand, reached maturity a few years later than he did, Italy would doubtless have made a different impression upon him; and his own sense of personal delicacy would have prevented him from writing the kind of literature that would have competed with the work of Theodore Dreiser, Sherwood Anderson, or Carl Sandburg. Writing at the exact time that he did, the last moment before the hold of the Genteel Tradition upon American culture was seriously challenged, Fuller could win applause for his Italian fiction from the older generation of Lowell and Norton and gain admiration for his Chicago novels from such younger men as Dreiser.

During his lifetime, of course, Fuller could not see the significance of his life and work in the perspective of cultural history. Throughout his most productive years, however, he lived painfully aware of his inability to commit himself fully or, as it were, even to choose between the line of development represented by Howells and that epitomized by Henry James, between realism and idealism, between Chicago and Italy. In each instance, he assented intellectually to the first alternative, yet he felt an emotional commitment to the second. During the best years of his career, he only partially solved this dilemma by writing first of Italy and then of Chicago but embodying essentially the same criticism of Chicago in all that he wrote. The bifurcation is more apparent than real, for Fuller's basic position remained constant for most of his career.

The happiest and most creative years of Fuller's life ended at the turn of the century with the failure of his hopes for the "upward movement" of art in Chicago, with his despondency over the role of American democracy in the Philippines, with his disappointment at the meager audience for his books, and, perhaps most of all, with his failure to recapture in middle life the freshness of his youthful response to Italy. Fuller decided, wisely it now seems, to write no more novels; and, for many years, he held to this decision. In the meantime, he seemed to live his life vicariously by spending his creative energies to advance the literary careers of his friends. Eventually, in the last decade of his life, Fuller viewed Chicago with a measure of acceptance, but by that time he had nothing compelling to say to the post-World War I generation.

Today, no student of American culture during the 1890's can afford to exclude Fuller from consideration. The recent reissue of one of his Chicago novels by a large university press indicates the continuing relevance of his work. Admittedly, he does not now rank as a major writer; nevertheless, he has a secure place, historically, in the development of American realism and in the area of American literary relations with Italy. In an important period in American history, Fuller made a valid criticism of American life and art; and he phrased his criticism in works which exhibit a high degree of literary craftsmanship.

Not to "revive" Fuller but to illuminate both the man and his literary work has been the primary objective of this book. In the accomplishment of this purpose, Fuller's complex personality has been viewed in relation to the persons, places, and ideas that were meaningful to him. Within this context Fuller's major literary production has been summarized and critically evaluated. Only the least significant of his magazine and newspaper articles, short stories, and book reviews have been excluded on the ground that even slight summarization and criticism of them would seriously limit the space essential for an adequate treatment of his major literary works.

JOHN PILKINGTON, JR.

University, Mississippi

Acknowledgments

I wish to express my appreciation to those persons who have helped to make this book a reality. To them is due much of the credit for whatever merits the volume may have, although they are in no way responsible for its deficiencies. In particular, I would acknowledge my debt to the following persons:

To Miss Helen Ranney, who gave me permission to quote passages from the unpublished papers of her uncle, Henry Blake Fuller, and to Mrs. Constance Garland Doyle and Mrs. Isabel Garland Lord, who have permitted me to quote passages from unpublished work of their father, Hamlin Garland.

To Mrs. Amy Nyholm, Manuscript Librarian, and the staff of the Newberry Library for permission to use the Fuller Collection and to quote passages from Fuller's manuscripts.

To Mr. Lloyd A. Arvidson, Curator of the American Literature Collection of the University of Southern California, for permission to use the Garland Collection and to quote passages from Fuller's correspondence with Hamlin Garland.

To Dr. J. E. Pomfret, Director, and Mr. Herbert C. Schulz, Curator of Manuscripts, the Henry E. Huntington Library, for permission to quote passages from the diaries of Hamlin Garland.

To Mr. W. H. Bond, Librarian, the Houghton Library, Harvard University, for permission to quote passages from Fuller's letters in the Howells Collection.

To Miss Margaret Scriven, Librarian, and Mr. Archie Motley, Manuscript Librarian, Chicago Historical Society, for permission to use the Fuller material in the library.

To my colleagues in the humanities, especially Professor Clare L. Marquette, I am grateful for many helpful comments. Mrs. Oscar R. Feagin, Mrs. J. D. Johnson, and Mr. Thomas W. Tullos, members of the staff of the library of the University of Mississippi, have rendered assistance in various ways.

I wish to acknowledge my general indebtedness to Constance Griffin's early biographical study about Fuller and to the excellent doctoral dissertations by Bernard R. Bowron, Kenny Jackson, Richard A. Pearce, and Paul Rosenblatt. I greatly appreciate the helpfulness of Sylvia E. Bowman in the preparation for publication of this my second book in the series of which she is editor.

Grants from the Faculty Research Committee of the University of Mississippi have provided a portion of the expense of the research and relieved me from teaching duties for parts of the summer session.

My greatest debt is to my wife, Lillian, whose interest and encouragement helped me to write the book and whose editorial and typing skills corrected more errors than I like to remember.

Contents

Contents

Chronology

1857   Henry Blake Fuller born January 9, Chicago.

1872   Attends the South Division High School, Chicago.

1873–   Becomes a student at the Allison Classical Academy,
1874   Oconomowoc, Wisconsin.

1875–   Resumes studies at the South Division High School;
1876   after graduation is employed at Ovington's Crockery.

1878   During employment at the Home National Bank, saves
money for trip abroad.

1879   August 17, begins the pilgrimage to Italy.

1880   Returns to Chicago after a year in Europe.

1883   In April, leaves for second tour of Europe; returns to
Boston in September.

1884   Publishes first humorous and satirical pieces in *Life;*
early contributions to Chicago *Tribune.*

1885   Death of Fuller's father; Fuller writes "Howells or
James?"

1886   Begins to write *The Chevalier of Pensieri-Vani.*

1890   Under pseudonym "Stanton Page" publishes *The Chevalier of Pensieri-Vani.*

1892   January 5, sails for Europe on his third trip abroad,
after preparing *The Chatelaine of La Trinité* for serialization in *The Century Magazine* and publication by the
Century Company; returns to Chicago in June; and
writes articles about the architecture of the World's
Columbian Exposition.

1893   *The Cliff-Dwellers* published.

1894   Completes *With the Procession* in the spring; begins
lifelong friendship with Hamlin Garland; makes fourth
trip to Italy; returns to Chicago late in October.

1895   *With the Procession* published in May.

1896   After *The Puppet-Booth* is published, sails on fifth trip
to Europe; itinerary to include Africa and Italy.

1897   Travels in Sicily and Italy; translates Italian stories;
reads widely in contemporary Italian fiction; returns to

Chicago in June; "The Upward Movement in Chicago" published in *Atlantic Monthly.*

1898 *From the Other Side* published.

1899 Reacts strongly to American conduct in the Philippines in *The New Flag: Satires;* becomes pessimistic over the plight of the arts and the artist in America; begins *The Last Refuge.*

1900– Writes editorials for *The Saturday Evening Post* and
1901 contributes articles to the Chicago *Post;* satirical novelettes, *Under the Skylights,* published.

1902– Conducts weekly literary supplement to Chicago *Evening*
1903 *Post.*

1908 *Waldo Trench and Others* published.

1910– Writes editorials and short feature articles for the Chicago
1914 *Record Herald.*

1912 Becomes member of the advisory committee for *Poetry: A Magazine of Verse.*

1916 Writes "A New Field for Free Verse" for *The Dial.*

1917 Free-verse experiments published as *Lines Long and Short;* writes "A Plea for Shorter Novels" and review articles for *The Dial.*

1918 *On the Stairs,* autobiographical novel, published.

1919 *Bertram Cope's Year* published.

1921– Writes general articles on literary subjects for *The Free-*
1924 *man, The New Republic, The Nation,* and other important periodicals.

1924 Makes sixth and final trip to Italy.

1929 Writes *Gardens of This World* and *Not on the Screen,* and begins a final novel; dies July 29.

CHAPTER 1

The Business of Life Inaugurated

The strange juxtaposition of Chicago and Italy in the life and writings of Henry Blake Fuller startled both the literary expert and the layman of his generation. Almost no one would have thought it conceivable that a writer from the raw, vulgar city of Chicago could write so charmingly of the postroads of Tuscany that, in cultured Boston, Charles Eliot Norton and James Russell Lowell would agree that this unknown Midwestern author had literary genius. Even less would anyone in 1890 have predicted that, shortly after writing a second romantic idyll of Europe, this same author would produce a novel about middle-class life in Chicago that William Dean Howells would acclaim as a superb piece of realism. The sudden appearance of a genius from Chicago was astonishing; the combination in his work of Italy and Chicago, of romance and realism, was even more remarkable.

I   The Shaping Forces

Of these seemingly disparate elements, the most important, in fact, the common denominator of Henry Blake Fuller's entire career, is Chicago. The city and its history must always constitute the frame of reference from which Fuller's life and literary work are measured. Chicago shaped his career; Chicago gave form to his basic attitudes; and Chicago provided the focal point for his literary and artistic endeavors.

In 1857, when Fuller was born, Chicago was still a small town whose more prosperous inhabitants, including Fuller's family, had only recently migrated from New England. As a boy of fourteen, he was an eyewitness to the greatest single event in the history of Chicago—the devastating fire of 1871. As a young man, seeking a start in life, he observed firsthand the amazing rapidity with which the population of the city reached the million mark. As a professional man of letters, he saw the beginnings and the climax of the "upward movement" of the arts in the decade of the 1890's; and as a lonely man in his sixties, he contemplated the post-World War I changes in the city as he evaluated its past. Throughout his lifetime, Fuller never ceased to maintain and to increase his minute knowledge of the city. On such matters as the history and architecture of its buildings, the layout of the streets and alleys, the boundaries of the parks, and the details of suburban additions, Fuller made himself an authority. Although he often spoke as if he hated the city, he never ceased to respect it and never left it for any considerable period of time. His major point of reference is Chicago.

The great fire of 1871 divides the history of Chicago into two sharply distinguished periods. The old Chicago dates from the incorporation of the town in 1833 and the exclusion of the Indians two years later; it ends dramatically with the virtual destruction of the city in the holocaust. Between these two dates, its salient features were phenomenal growth and the conviction of leading citizens that Chicago would one day become the greatest city in the Midwest, perhaps even the greatest city in the nation. They justified their faith in the future largely upon Chicago's position at the junction of the eastern terminus of the Erie Canal and the Mississippi River, the nation's greatest inland waterway. They knew that the trade and commerce across the continent both east and west, as well as north and south, would flow through this city. The population statistics validate their expectations. By 1840, the original population of one hundred persons had increased to four thousand; ten years later the city numbered thirty thousand; and by 1860, when the population had climbed above one hundred thousand, Chicago was no longer a town but a mushrooming city. In 1870, the year before the fire, when the figure was almost three hundred thousand, the city seemed moving rapidly towards becoming a major metropolis. What happened later—the history of Chicago as a metropolis and then a cosmopolis—belongs to the new or modern phase of the city's development.

Necessarily, the culture of old Chicago was largely a transplant from the East. A large segment of its population, and almost all of its leading citizens, had moved westward from New England and New York, although a few, for example, Cyrus McCormick and the first Carter Harrison, had come from the South. Representative of the intellectual, moral, and religious traditions of the eastern seaboard, they consciously and unconsciously subscribed to the cultural values of the Genteel Tradition. For the most part, however, they were primarily interested in amassing fortunes; and during the decades of the 1850's, 1860's, and even 1870's, they were inclined to live simply, spending long hours at their places of business and devoting little or none of their energies to social and cultural affairs.

After 1870, when the population of Chicago doubled itself twice in the two succeeding decades, the character of the city and its leadership changed remarkably. By 1890, the foreign population had enormously increased; industrial development had reached undreamed of proportions; and successive real estate booms, always a factor in Chicago's growth, had altered the face of the now huge and ugly city. Accompanying this new Chicago were new values, new standards, and new leaders; and few recognized or felt more profoundly than Henry Blake Fuller the differences between the old Chicago and the city that was rapidly emerging. As a young man, his attitudes toward such matters as religion, ethics, culture, and the good life had been shaped by the tenets of the Genteel Tradition. In his maturity, he found himself unprepared and temperamentally unwilling to meet the competition of the new city. He became actively hostile to the new philosophy of big business, the law of the jungle, or the Frank Cowperwood formula of "I satisfy myself." There were moments when he became an alien in his own city; yet he always identified himself with it. As he often said, "I was born and brought up in Chicago, and there I belong."[1] Much, though not all, of his life and his literary work may be explained in these terms.

II A Chicago Childhood

From the arrival of Dr. Samuel Fuller (1580-1633) aboard the *Mayflower* to the early years of the nineteenth century, the Fuller family had lived in New England where its members produced a long line of prominent ministers, physicians, and soldiers. Henry Blake Fuller's grandfather, Judge Henry Fuller (1805-79), who was to become one of the "old settlers" of Chicago, was a cousin of Margaret Fuller Ossoli. In 1830, at the age of twenty-five, he left his birthplace in Northampton, Massachusetts, to migrate westward. After engaging in business as a tanner in Wyoming, New York, and later as a drygoods merchant in Albion, New York, he became a county judge in St. Joseph, Michigan. In 1848, he settled in Chicago, where his finances improved so rapidly that within the next several decades he made a considerable fortune from his activities in the Rock Island and West Chicago City Railroad systems and from the development of the Chicago water system. Judge Fuller remained until his death a New Englander. Neither wealth nor the urban conditions of life in Chicago altered an outlook and a behavior essentially austere, individualistic, conservative, and provincial.

Henry Blake Fuller's father, George Wood Fuller (1832-83), who was born in Lockport, New York, inherited the conservative New England family tradition which Judge Fuller had brought westward to Chicago. George Fuller married Mary Josephine Sanford (1836-1907) whose family had migrated in the seventeenth century from England to Massachusetts and thence to Connecticut. For a time he was secretary of the Southside Railway Company and afterwards its vice-president. Lacking the inclination, or perhaps the ability or energy, to make money by striking out for himself, he conserved rather than expanded the family fortune. After Judge Fuller died, George Fuller suffered financial reverses, and, by the time his son undertook the management of the estate, the sizable financial holdings of Judge Fuller had notably diminished. Years after his father's death, Henry Blake Fuller included a sketch of George Fuller in the thinly disguised autobiographical novel, *On the Stairs*. Substituting the name James Prince for that of his father, Fuller wrote: "I gathered, later, that James Prince had done little, unaided, for himself; whatever he had accomplished had been in conjunction with other men. . . . To him fell the property—and its worries. The worries, I surmise, were the greater part of it all" (24). The comment may be accepted as Fuller's estimate of his father's career.

Fuller's attitude toward his family tends to obscure the fact that his father and grandfather were substantial citizens of Chicago and that, among the "old settlers," they counted as a force in the community. Fuller's own temperament, tastes, and ambitions had nothing in common with those of his father or his grandfather; they came to stand as typical of much that Fuller hated in the city of Chicago. The influence of his mother, like that of his father and grandfather, was, in a sense, a negative one; and the atmosphere in the home increased, even if it did not actually produce, Fuller's introspective way of life. In his early diaries, Fuller rarely mentioned his mother, who was an invalid, except occasionally to record that she had departed for or returned from "Coonie," his name for the resort area of Oconomowoc, Wisconsin.

As a man, Fuller maintained an almost complete silence about his family. Not even his most intimate friends felt that they knew his circumstances. Hamlin Garland, for example, in whose home Fuller visited, often for weeks at a time, for more than thirty-five years, never learned any of the details or events of Fuller's youth. In 1901, Garland wrote in his diary that Fuller's youth remained "remote, cold, shadowy" (November 15, 1901); and, on the occasion of Fuller's mother's death in 1907, Garland entered the Fuller home for the first and probably the last time. Garland's entry in his diary for this day is revealing: "We went to the funeral of Fuller's mother today and it was a glimpse into his origin to see the walls of this home" (October 10, 1907).

Despite Fuller's silence about his immediate family in Chicago, he could, at times, be very talkative about his New England ancestry. The reason is apparent in the contrast between the Chicago Fuller knew and the New England he imagined. In New England, Fuller believed that there was an atmosphere favorable to culture, learning, and the arts; a sense of the past; an established tradition; a respect for the integrity of the individual. In Chicago, he was inclined to doubt the existence of any of these conditions; what was always most real in the Midwest was an ever increasing commercialism and a corresponding vulgarity. He never seems to have realized that his parents were in any way responsible for his New England preferences. On the contrary, Fuller, from his earliest childhood, may have judged that his father and grandfather had succumbed to the commercialism of Chicago; and, as between Chicago and New England, it was in New England, from whence his ancestors had come, that the free and artistic spirit best flourished in America. Fuller, therefore, claimed allegiance to New England and liked to have it said that he was essentially a New Englander.

The meager information available about Fuller's childhood, from his birth, January 9, 1857, in a house that stood on the site of the present La Salle Street Station, until his twelfth year, reveals him as a very shy, retiring boy who instead of playing outdoors with the neighborhood children chose such indoor and solitary amusements as knitting and piano playing.[2] So early as 1868, when Fuller was attending the Moseley School, he began to save various mementoes of his school days. Prominent among them are his report cards which show him as an excellent student, consistently ranking first, second, or third in the class.

Among the papers which Fuller kept is a notebook, or diary, covering the school year 1871-72, his final year at the Moseley School. It furnishes abundant evidence of Fuller's pressing desire to compete academically with his schoolmates. In his only reference to the Chicago fire which had occurred just a month before he began the diary, Fuller noted that "since the 'cow kicked'" he had ranked first in his class on six occasions. His concern, amounting to anxiety, to stand well in his class is evident from the first entry he made: "I feel very joyous this morning, because I stood 98 last week in school. This is a good start for the month, and the month may be a good start for the medal, at the end of the year." When he was graduated in June, 1872, his year's average was slightly higher than ninety-eight. Noting the fact in the diary, Fuller exclaimed: "How is that for high!" He won a First Medal; and, in the entrance examination for the Chicago High School, Fuller was one of three boys scoring ninety-one, the highest mark attained.

In the fall of 1872, Fuller entered the Chicago High School; but, after the first week of school, he transferred to the Branch South Division High School, which he attended during the academic year 1872-73. Although Fuller's diaries and notebooks do not include this period, his parents' abrupt decision to take him out of the public school and to enter him in a private academy strengthens the inference that Fuller's first year at the South Division High School was an unhappy experience.

III   At the Allison Academy

During the fall and spring semesters of the school year 1873-74, Fuller attended the Allison Classical Academy at Oconomowoc. Later he characterized his experience there as the "happiest year of my life"[3] and incorporated many of his memories of the school in his novels, *On the Stairs* and *Bertram Cope's Year,* and in the unfinished story of "Edmund Dalrymple." Although Fuller's diaries and notebooks from the year at the Allison supply the reasons for his happiness at the school, significantly, intellectual stimulus cannot be included among them.

Intellectual activity at the Allison Classical Academy was held to a minimum. Fuller was quick to perceive that the members of the faculty—consisting of the Reverend J. Allison, who had founded the school in the preceding year, his wife, son, and one other teacher—were by no means the intellectual equivalents of the instructors he had encountered in the Chicago schools. His attitude toward the faculty is evident from his ironic comment following a class in geometry: "I think at the conclusion of the recitation, Mr. Allison fully understood the subject." The strenuous academic competition which Fuller had known in Chicago must have been totally absent in Oconomowoc.

What made Fuller remember the school with pleasure was the fact that at the academy he enjoyed a degree of social acceptance from the other boys that he had never known in Chicago. At the Allison, Fuller lived with five other boys on the upstairs floor of a small "cottage" near the main building. Assigned two to a room, they remained undisturbed by the young "Doc" Allison who slept below on the ground floor. Four of these boys soon formed the "Jolly Quartette" and began to hold their spreads in Fuller's room. Remembering these affairs, Fuller wrote: "I can think of the quartette meetings only with pleasure, and regret that they are forever passed. But of my whole school life at the Allison, these convivial noctures were my greatest trial. Quiet and privacy were invaded, study was entirely prevented, bedtime and sleep thoughtlessly disregarded. A room full of stifling heat, and boys, and smoke, and noise. How vividly I can recall my sufferings!" Fuller's complaints of the messiness of his room—the "unwashed stewpans, scattered packs of cards and old cigar stumps . . . paper bags, oyster cans and a multitude of interesting commodities"—were doubtless real and justified; but the fact that a short time later he could remember these incidents with delight underscores their real significance.

In retrospect, Fuller took pleasure in the realization that, for once in his life, he had become a participant in a group, even if not a full participant. Fuller never actually belonged to the "Jolly Quartette," and he never could bring himself to eat oysters, smoke cigars, or play poker. Still, he was included. He could not have been called popular; and there were many times when he was not accepted at all, when he felt, as he said, "most heartlessly and cruelly snubbed."

To a few students, for example, Frank L. Donaldson, who never snubbed him, Fuller felt particularly drawn. Donaldson, a Brooklyn boy, a year or two older than most of the students, kept a horse and "T-cart" at the local livery stable, exhibited an open contempt for the curriculum of the academy, and persistently endeavored to influence both boys and girls to join him in his pursuit of pleasure. Gregarious, sophisticated, and unintellectual, Donaldson was everything Fuller was not; but Donaldson's interest in singing provided a bond between them. In his recollections of the Allison Academy, Fuller noted that Donaldson "took great delight in performing secundo to several of my airs, and our duets became justly celebrated. . . . But our pièce par excellence was the Che la morte from Trovatore; this was his especial favorite, and at all times of the day I was besieged to play it with him." Years later, these incidents provided Fuller with considerable material for scenes in *Bertram Cope's Year* and for "Edmund Dalrymple."

Although more than a fourth of the boarding students at the academy were girls, Fuller, then approaching seventeen, showed little interest in the opposite sex. While members of the Jolly Quartette and his own roommate successfully engaged in youthful romances with Flora Van Nostrand, the most popular girl in school, Fuller remained aloof, indifferent, even hostile. Uninterested in her as a young woman, he resented the time, attention, and affection that she drew from those he desired as his friends.⁴ Fuller's attitude toward her presaged his relationship with women for the remainder of his life; he knew them only upon an intellectual and platonic basis.

Notwithstanding the disturbing note that Flora's presence introduced or the occasions upon which he was either snubbed or ignored, Fuller was happy at the academy. By ceasing to compete anxiously for grade points, he began to enjoy his studies, especially his Latin course. If the quality of instruction left much to be desired, the relaxed atmosphere of the classrooms and his easy comradeship with the other pupils were ample compensations. His musical talents, his participation in the debating society, and his editorship of a highly successful, if shortlived, school paper represented activities that both gave him a sense of personal accomplishment and added distinctly to his standing in the school. For most of the time, in fact, Fuller had substantial reasons for believing himself respected, recognized, and, at times, admired.

Fuller never again attained the same degree of identification with a group of persons or with a cause as he did at Oconomowoc, and for the remainder of his life he fought loneliness. It is little wonder that he called this year the happiest in his life and that time and again, long after the school had disappeared, Fuller, amidst his unhappiness, desired to return to "Coonie," where he had attended the Allison Classical Academy.

IV The Business of Life

When Fuller left the Allison, he still lacked at least a year of finishing high school. By all expectations he should have either returned to the academy in the fall or reentered the South Division High School. The terse entry, dated September 21, 1874, in a new diary which he had begun the preceding summer, therefore, comes as a surprise: "The 'business of life' formally inaugurated. Ovington's—Crockery—122 State St."⁵ Fuller had joined thousands of other young boys in Chicago on the long climb that led from the bottom of the business ladder toward financial success at the top.

Fuller, then approaching eighteen, was hardly a promising

candidate for business success. No one who knew him would have predicted that he would succeed as a clerk in a "crockery" store. At the time he took this position, Fuller was assiduously engaged in translating Schiller and Goethe into blank verse, in making himself "a master of the English tongue," and in developing his powers of "character sketching."[6] Long before breakfast in the mornings, Fuller was at work on his studies, feeding his own intellectual furnace and feeding it in his own way.[7] For the winter his self-designed curriculum included attendance at as many operas and plays as possible and the reading of such literary works as Dickens' novels, Johnson's *Rasselas*, and Gibbon's *The Decline and Fall of the Roman Empire*. His eagerness at this age to undertake this tough, highly intellectual program reflects Fuller's passion for self-improvement and provides an index to his real interests. While these subjects occupied his mind, he would hardly find the commercial atmosphere of Ovington's congenial or, more likely, even tolerable.

Even if Fuller's tastes and interests had not been antithetical to the values of the marketplace, his personality would have effectively precluded him from an occupation which required frequent contact with the public. In one of his moments of introspection, Fuller wrote that "it is my misfortune to appear diffident and embarrassed at those very times when I should most appear of an easy and graceful deportment." He felt this embarrassment even among persons of his own age. "I have mingled very little in society—the society, of course, of young people," wrote Fuller. "I have had little desire for it; often a dislike—more, a positive aversion."[8]

Both Fuller's desire for privacy and his aversion to meeting people were intensified by his speech difficulties. For several years, he had thought that rapid reading caused him to speak so rapidly that his pronunciation became garbled. The greater attention Fuller paid to the niceties of language, written and oral, the more self-conscious he became; and, as his self-consciousness increased, his speech defects became even more apparent. He found himself in a vicious circle. The consequence was that, to use Fuller's words, "I positively fear to undertake a moderately long sentence; short expressions form my conversation. I begin a sentence with great velocity—stumble—repeat—make, and this is the unkindest cut of all, a grammatical error—an error in pronunciation—and finish in utter confusion. With the utmost pain I am slowly improving, and in time may learn to speak my mother tongue with facility and intelligibility."[9] By great effort, Fuller eventually improved his speech, although to the end of his life he spoke with a deliberation that his hearers often mistook for affectation. In the meantime, the speech handicap made his position at Ovington's all the more distasteful to him.

As the weeks passed, Fuller's unhappiness at the store increased. On January 10, 1875, his eighteenth birthday, he wrote in his diary that he would always think of himself at this age "as a boy in bad health, and who wished to be somewhere else."[10] By March, he had had all he could stand of work at Ovington's, and in an entry entitled "a voice from the tombs," he declared: "I have done at last what I ought to have done weeks and weeks ago. I have spoken with reference to a return to Coonie. I leave Ovington's, and go for a few weeks at least to Coonie."

By securing his parents' consent for him to leave Ovington's and return to Oconomowoc, Fuller had taken an important step. He had voiced his opposition to a business career; and, at the same time, he had brought out into the open his desire to return to school. Except for study, Fuller had as yet nothing definite to propose as an alternative to Ovington's; yet his parents could hardly have been ignorant of the fact that he was spending all of his free time in study and writing. By permitting Fuller to return to Coonie and by subsequently allowing him to reenter the South Division High School, they seriously weakened any hope they may have held of channeling Fuller's energies and talents into business.

On arrival at Oconomowoc, Fuller heard that the Allison Classical Academy had been permanently closed. He was bitterly disappointed. After longing for months to return, it all seemed, as he confided to his diary, "a wild goose chase after happiness." He found a measure of consolation in the fact that Mrs. Allison was still available to help him with his studies; and, a few weeks later, when he returned to Chicago, his outlook was more cheerful than it had been during the past year.

In the fall of 1875, Fuller reentered the South Division High

School for his final year. Without attempting to repeat the competitive spirit he had displayed earlier at the Moseley School, Fuller distinguished himself with high marks; his over-all average for the two semesters was ninety-eight. Intellectually, he had advanced considerably beyond most high-school students. In addition to his knowledge of Latin literature, Fuller had read widely in the English, German, and French classics. He was a trained musician and an advanced student of musical composition. Finally, he could write English with a precision and a maturity of style characteristic of a professional writer. These outstanding academic and artistic achievements add significance to Fuller's brief entry in his diary for June 23, 1876: "Our Commencement. My school days probably over for aye."

It was only a question of time until Fuller would find for himself the particular field of art which he would choose for his major interest. He was, in fact, already moving toward the choice when he began a new diary a month after his graduation. In it he wrote: "For some time past, I have felt the need of some appropriate receptacle in which to group my flowers of rhetoric and fruits of thought. Mental activity I regard as essential to my existence, and I am so often nearly prostrated by the furor scribendi, that I have at last purchased this book, in the hope, that by giving proper vent to my thoughts and fancies, I may be able to prolong for a little my so seriously threatened life."[11] What he would write would be in large measure an expression of the opposition between the values of art and those of the marketplace. Although he was to cast his allegiance with art, there were times when it, too, would seem only "a wild goose chase after happiness."

CHAPTER 2

Towards a Definition of Civilization

Had Fuller been challenged by the opportunities of Chicago in the 1870's, he would have joined thousands of his contemporaries in the race to make money. Chicagoans expected every young man—the sooner, the better—to devote all of his energies and initiative either to making his own fortune or to expanding the one already made by his father. In a city devoted energetically to the widening of its boundaries, the increase of its capital, and the multiplication of its industry, the only kind of success that was recognized was a financial one. To the alert, intelligent, and vigorous young man bent on establishing a place for himself, Chicago offered vast opportunities and golden rewards. No one could even imagine a young man not wishing to compete in the race.

I Preparations

The path for Fuller was plainly marked: he had merely to fit into the pattern of Chicago life to succeed. His grandfather and his father expected him to compete, first at Ovington's and later in some more spectacular enterprise; and they certainly anticipated no serious opposition. What else could a young man do in Chicago? Only Fuller himself knew the depth of his dislike of business and the strength of his desire to seek the satisfactions of art. For the present, however, Fuller had no alternative. After graduation from high school, he must return to Ovington's. The entry in his diary is brief but pointed: "Back at the treadmill."[1]

For almost a year Fuller worked as a clerk among the glass and crockery at Ovington's. He performed his assignments capably, yet to him they remained only routine tasks to be accomplished each day before he was free to return to his room where he could pursue the studies that were meaningful to him. He had no ambitions at Ovington's; the work there was merely a job. Day by day his distaste for the work, the atmosphere, and the merchandise mounted until the day came when he could write in his diary: "Set free from daily contact with the things I loathe! Ovington's adieu, I pray, forever" (September 29, 1877). But after a six weeks' vacation at his favorite "Coonie," he went back to work as a messenger in the Bank of Illinois. Eight months later, in June, 1878, he was transferred to the Home National Bank where his father was vice-president. Fuller would work there almost a year.

During the years immediately following his graduation from high school, Fuller determined to free himself at least for a year, if not permanently, from Chicago. He wanted to travel in Europe to see for himself what civilization in its highest form could give the willing student. At night, in his room in his father's house, he could learn only so much of what there was to see and to feel; for the rest, he must make the pilgrimage to Europe. Cooper, Longfellow, Margaret Fuller, Hawthorne, Howells, James—and Mark Twain—had preceded him. Fuller resolved to follow in their footsteps. None of them went with higher hopes and greater enthusiasm than he, and none made more earnest preparations or laid more elaborate plans for the journey than Fuller. The really significant difference between Fuller and his predecessors lay in the fact that Fuller started from Chicago and returned to Chicago.

While working in the bank to secure the money to finance his Grand Tour, Fuller devoted most of his evenings to a thorough study of architecture. In an undated entry in his diary, he pictured himself as "drawing book after book on Architecture from the Library, transferring architectural designs to various slips of paper, penciling elevations of Gothic cathedrals, and in twenty different ways ministering to my present grande passion."[2] The longer he studied the subject, the more convinced he became that architecture provided the best key to the secrets of European civilization.

Fuller's devotion to architecture exercised a far more pervasive influence upon his writing than his interest in music. Although he played the piano with great skill, composed operettas, and served frequently as a music critic, music never suggested to him a method or principle of writing. Architecture, however, he always tended to associate with writing. In an un-published essay on "Architecture in America," he once asked: "How does a hurried editor judge of a bulky manuscript novel? Must he read the whole before he can form an opinion? On the contrary, he frequently spares himself this labor, and rightly, by running over a sheet selected here and there at random—no general survey is necessary. Can the writer, he asks, use the tools of his trade? *Does he know how to put words together?* So with a building; a bit will serve as well as the whole. Does the architect know how to put *his* words together—brick, stone, iron, glass, terra-cotta, what not? Can he write in the ver-nacular?"

Fuller was not satisfied merely with establishing an analogy between architecture and writing. Architecture, properly under-stood, Fuller wrote in the same essay, enabled one to reach "a mastery of style itself—of general style, of style absolute." The greatest achievement, explained Fuller, is "not to master *a* style, but to master—a much broader and more basic thing—style itself, style absolute." To Fuller "style absolute" in writing meant not only the careful selection of words to convey evenly the desired tone and the precise shade of meaning but also the balance and harmony of each part of a work with every other part. Without using the term, he was actually insisting upon organicism, an esthetic principle which he implied in the exhortation: "Let us take our stand . . . upon the lasting verities, upon the fundamental proprieties; let us place our dependence upon right feeling and straight thinking." To perfect this "right feeling and straight thinking," Fuller went to Europe.

In addition to his study of architecture, Fuller's prepara-tion for his trip abroad included an almost incredibly meticulous analysis of European maps and guidebooks. He made plan after plan, calculated distances and time-schedules down to the small-est fractions, and determined precisely where he would go, what he would see, and how long he would remain in each city and each country. His final itinerary, completed after enormous labor, and, ironically, altered repeatedly after the journey began, represented his zeal to gain the utmost from the trip. Fuller was no mere tourist travelling haphazardly wherever whim or a guide might lead him. He knew what he wanted to see: he wanted to see everything; there might not be another opportunity. Fuller never seems to have considered the possibility that one might prepare too carefully or that too much attention to the guidebooks might make him susceptible to advanced judgments and vitiate the element of surprise.

II England

On August 17, 1879, Henry Blake Fuller left Chicago bound for Europe on a year's journey of discovery. Three days later he was aboard the Cunard liner, S. S. *Scythia,* sailing for Liverpool, and already he was writing in his notebook a day-by-day account of his experiences. By following this practice throughout his travels, Fuller filled, in his precise, meticulous autograph, three large notebooks before his return a year later.

After a dull, uneventful voyage, Fuller landed at Liverpool, August 30, 1879. The beginning was inauspicious, for he found the city substantially like American cities. "Take lower New York," he wrote, "improve the pavements; make the new buildings not quite so fine, and the old ones a good deal shabbier, and all somewhat more sombre and substantial; throw in a few cabs and a few policemen of a certain cut, and a good number of shabby men, frowsy women and uncared for children, and you have a pretty fair idea of Liverpool without much trouble."[3] For a pilgrim with the high hopes and great expectations that Fuller held, this first glimpse of Old World civilization was neither rewarding nor promising.

After leaving Liverpool, Fuller visited Chester, Chatsworth Palace, Haddon Hall, Lichfield, Coventry, Warwick Castle, Kenilworth, Stratford-on-Avon, Oxford, and London. At Chester he could be enthusiastic over the ancient walls of the city, and at Chatsworth Palace he found much to praise. Fuller, however, was by no means pleased with everything; at Oxford, for example, he found the university buildings "so horribly discolored, so shockingly decayed, as to be almost ghastly" (September 6, 1879).

On September 7, Fuller reached London, and for the next three weeks, he tirelessly explored the sights of the city. After making his pilgrimage to what he called the "marble jungle" of Westminster Abbey, Fuller remarked upon "the atrocious taste displayed in the monuments and sculpture generally."

"What other place," asked Fuller, "can show so rank and hideous a growth of monumental monstrosities?" Despite his criticism, Fuller returned again and again to Westminster during his stay in London. He had little regard for St. Paul's which he described as "Wren's great classic sham" (September 16, 1879). Dutifully, he inspected most of the notable attractions of the English capital. He spent hours wandering through the British Museum, the Guildhall, and the Houses of Parliament. At the National Gallery he had to admit failure, noting in his journal that "I had to give it up—the Old Masters are too many for me" (September 13, 1879). Always, architecture was more significant to Fuller than painting.

Day after day, Fuller recorded in his notebook the places he had seen: Prince Albert's Crystal Palace, Kew, Richmond, Hampton Court, the Zoological Gardens, the South Kensington Museum, Hyde Park, Greenwich, Chancery Lane, Window, Eton, Gravesend. At night, when he returned to his room to prepare his daily essay, he was exhausted. Almost with a sigh of relief, Fuller reached the end of his London itinerary; and, after spending a day mending his clothes, he crossed into France.

Although Fuller never openly admitted any dissatisfaction with his tour of England, the entries in his notebook lack enthusiasm. Part of the explanation may lie in the fact that Fuller, strongly influenced by the architectural theories of John Ruskin, disliked many of the architectural monuments he saw in England. In addition, Fuller's inexperience as a traveller may have been a factor. Undoubtedly, he attempted to see too much in the time at his disposal; and he had not yet learned to overcome the temptation constantly to compare what he saw with its counterpart in America. Later, when he set himself a more leisurely pace and freed himself, to a degree at least, of the American measuring rod, he began to enjoy his journey and to broaden his taste.

III France

In France, where his tour was confined almost wholly to Paris, Fuller saved money by living in a garret and by eating in a restaurant where the food was cheap. He even purchased a supply of candles to prevent his landlord from overcharging him for lighting. Three weeks after his arrival, he changed his lodgings to a pension in the Latin Quarter, asserting that "je commençais d'avoir peur de la mechante Marie aux yeux noirs" (October 23, 1879). More likely, Fuller's sudden change of address was due mainly to his wish to keep his whereabouts secret. His fondness for privacy, especially in regard to his living quarters, appeared early in his career and increased as he became older until it amounted virtually to an obsession.

Fuller was rapidly learning how to cover ground and how to make use of his experiences in his writing. The section of the notebook devoted to Paris represents a noticeable improvement upon the account of his visit to England. Because of his interest in architecture, Fuller's remarks primarily concern the cathedrals and public buildings of Paris; but he is more confident of himself, has a better grasp of what makes a good subject for writing, and understands the importance of variety.

Fuller's entry for October 11, 1879, reflects these improvements. He began with a recital of the day's sightseeing: "I have done the whole Cité—except the Morgue!—and done it pretty thoroughly, too. Notre Dame twice, inside, outside, front, back, and up to the top; the Sainte Chapelle, twice also; a stroll around through the Palais de Justice; an outside view of the Hotel Dieu; an inside view of the Tribunal de Commerce, with its fine staircase, a glance at the flower-market near by; and a general lounge along the quais and around the Pont Neuf." For almost any tourist except Fuller, this itinerary would have been fatiguing to the point of disaster; for Fuller it was by no means exceptional. Far from being fatigued, on that same evening he took a walk through the adjacent boulevards.

For the remainder of this entry in his journal, Fuller selected for extended comment only two of the places he had visited, Notre Dame and the Sainte Chapelle. He began his account by noting the general architectural features of the cathedral: "The front is the finest Gothic composition that I may ever hope to see, and the system of choir-buttresses is so bold and nervy as to approximate the sensational; the construction of the triforium is most lucid and logical, and the three rose windows are probably unrivaled in the gracefulness of their tracery and the gloriousness of their coloring. The ascent of the south tower gave me my fourth bird's-eye view of the city, and afforded a fine opportunity for the study of architectural details." At this point Fuller abruptly interrupted his discussion of architecture to relate a humorous experience arising from the language difficulties of Americans in France. Fuller became increasingly skillful in narrating the short anecdote set against an architectural background. He used the method repeatedly in writing his first book of fictional travel, *The Chevalier of Pensieri-Vani*.

The measure of Fuller's development as a writer, however, may best be seen in the concluding portion of this entry. After writing the anecdote about Notre Dame, he smoothly made a transition to Sainte Chapelle; and, as in the anecdote, the emphasis is not so much upon architecture as upon Fuller himself.

> The Sainte Chapelle is situated within the precincts of the Palais de Justice, and is shown by a municipal officer with all the neatness and dispatch that should mark the transaction of public business. You see Notre Dame as you wish; you see the Sainte Chapelle as they wish. You can ride rough shod over sacristans and beadles and acolytes and the inferior clergy,—in my most flushed and frenzied moments I have sometimes thought myself equal to running down an archbishop or cardinal—but you buckle down at once before a minion of the law, the state, the government. The custodian of the Sainte Chapelle is firm, inflexible, adamantine. You may inspect his charge a dozen times over, if you please, but you must do it in a brisk, orderly, time-table-y way. I felt that twice did the building abundant justice.

The subjectivity of Fuller's entries in the Paris section of his journal may owe something to his lack of sympathy with French painting, sculpture, and architecture. He was uncomfortable in the Louvre. Most of the paintings did not appeal to him either emotionally or intellectually, and the sculpture, one surmises, was too bold for Fuller's genteel taste. Although he would not have admitted a preference for draped figures, his attitude may be inferred from his remark, "I prefer to regard the Venus of Milo, not as a goddess of Love, but as a goddess in the abstract" (October 20, 1879).

He found Versailles "dull" and "hateful" (October 21, 1879). The park he described as "a mere armistice between art and nature in which both sides appear to decided disadvantage." The Trianon, wrote Fuller, is "blighted by that worldly, superficial elegance with which the French taint everything they touch," and he agreed with H. A. Taine, the French critic, that "though the French still possess the sense of elegance, they have quite lost the sense of beauty." His final verdict was that "the best thing about Versailles is leaving it." Versailles represented one of many excursions Fuller felt he must make before he could treat himself to the pleasure of Italy.

IV Rome

"What, after all, is civilization?" asked Fuller in his journal the night of his departure from France. Although the answer, Fuller thought, was more likely to be found in Rome than in Paris, he was in no hurry to reach the Italian capital. Before Rome, he wanted to explore Genoa, Pisa, Florence, Siena, and Orvieto. Crammed with cathedrals, churches, palazzos which in turn were filled with paintings, sculptures, and objects of art, these places proved to be all that Fuller had imagined them. He was delighted with Genoa, which he pronounced the most enjoyable place he had yet visited. In Florence, his genteel, Chicago-trained sensibilities were disturbed, of course, by the "evil of such promiscuous nudity as meets the eye at every turn in Florence" (November 26, 1879). As for the "Nude in Art," Fuller's refusal to be specific scarcely hid his disapproval. Despite the display of nudity in the sculptures and the paintings, and the rain which fell throughout most of his visit, Fuller derived immense satisfaction from his two weeks in Florence.

On December 6, 1879, Fuller arrived in Rome. "Did any writer," asked Fuller, "of any half-way respectable book of travel—and what am I if not a writer, and what is my book if not respectable?—ever fail to state just under what circumstances he first beheld the dome of St. Peter's or neglect to give the details of his entry into and first progress through the Eternal City?" (December 7, 1879). Replying to his own question, Fuller wrote: "His first glimpse of the dome of St. Peter's was caught from the rather dirty window of a rather crowded compartment of a second class railway-carriage, at the very moment when he held a—a *pulce* between the thumb and forefinger of his left hand and was wondering how he could dispose of the infliction without attracting the attention of his fellow-travelers."

The flea in Fuller's hand and the dome of St. Peter's suggest something more than contrasts in size and importance. Fuller could have made them symbolic of the two Italys which he never could reconcile: the Italy of the past, of art, of ancient "civilization"; and the Italy of filth, of poverty, of superstition.

For Fuller the goal of his pilgrimage was at hand. Day after day, for the next three months, in rain and cold, as well as in bright weather, he was determined to explore the city. He had come, as he said, "to know the Forum, the Capitol, the Palatine, the Velabrum, through and through, all around and all over." Long evenings spent in studying guidebooks before he left Chicago had fully prepared him for what he was to see; and, as Fuller walked toward the Coliseum on his first day in Rome, he knew what to expect: "I knew just where it was, and that I was about to see it" (December 10, 1879). His enthusiasm almost overwhelmed him. "My second day in Rome, with a glorious afternoon in the Forum," he wrote in his notebook. "I again crossed the Capitol, and repeating in a sort of solemn chant the stately paraphrase, 'This is the / Fo rum Ro / man um,' I descended the slight stairway leading down to that bit of classic soil, and spent some hours in a series of views from various standpoints—from the standpoint of the picturesque, the sentimental, the aesthetic and the historical" (December 11, 1879). Nothing was going to escape Fuller.

Rome, more than any other city, and Italy, more than any other country, gave Fuller a sense of being "abroad." It was utterly different from Chicago. In a moment of serious reflection, he analyzed his feelings: "There are certain points, situations, in Rome where the sense of 'being abroad,' of finding one's self actually and truly 'in Europe,' of receiving in full measure the aesthetic delights of Continental travel, of feeling that 'it is good to be here,' and that for *such* a combination of time and place and circumstance you have dreamt and waited a good many years, comes upon you with a strong and irresistible force" (January 4, 1880). Chicago seemed far, far away, almost in another universe.

In England, in France, and in Northern Italy, Fuller had already worked out the method of sightseeing that he would follow in Rome. He began with a series of walks throughout the main parts of the city, for he felt that his preliminary view was essential to give him a proper perspective. Afterwards, he selected particular sites for viewing, but he never remained more than an hour or two at any given place. To such famous attractions as the Vatican, the Forum, the Barberini Palace, the Coliseum, the Pincio, the Corso, the Borghese villa and gardens, Fuller returned again and again in order to see them from every possible vantage point and to fix them permanently in his mind. Others, like the Baths of Titus, the Catacombs, the Villa Ludovisi, and the Church of St. Cecilia, he saw but once. By February 20, 1880, he could record in his journal: "With the exception of some few odds and ends I have seen everything of Rome within the walls, and have lately been giving some attention to the sights beyond them." By March 7, he had seen all that he had time to see, perhaps not everything, but certainly all that careful planning, indefatigable walking, and an unquenchable thirst for sightseeing would allow him.

Despite his boundless enthusiasm for sightseeing, Fuller could not admire all that he saw in Rome. Most of the religious paintings, for example, he thought interesting historically but not esthetically. Of the hundreds of paintings and frescoes that he saw, only Guido Reni's *Aurora* gave him unmixed pleasure. As for architecture, his observation that "Italy has been telling architectural lies for three centuries" (December 10, 1879) indicates his attitude. His characteristic approach to many of the most famous buildings of Rome may be inferred from his remarks about St. Peter's: "Structurally, the only wholly admirable features of St. Peter's are the dome and the coffered ceiling of the nave—though the great vestibule is not without its good points. Aesthetically, St. Peter's is wholly pagan. Morally, St. Peter's is a glorification of a dis-christianized Papacy. As a building, St. Peter's is rather grandiose than grand; to call it a 'beautiful Christian temple of worship' is unadmissable, for it is neither beautiful nor Christian; to pronounce it a 'triumph of Catholic faith' is rankly absurd" (December 12, 1879). Fuller was sharply critical of almost every building that he saw in Rome, the only outstanding exception being the modern basilica of St. Paul which he described as "the most magnificent building in Rome or near it" (February 20, 1880). Inside the churches, he also found much to dislike: he time and again complained of the dirt, the omnipresent beggars, and the super-stitious veneration accorded the saints' relics.

Everywhere he went he saw the juxtaposition of the good and the bad, the old and the new, the genuine and the meretricious. Because it was a "most incongruous and extraordinary jumble of splendor and slovenliness, magnificence and meanness," Fuller considered the Sistine Chapel "characteristically Roman" (December 23, 1879). In support of his judgment, he continued: "The floor is typical of the whole: one half is of Opus Alexandrinum, the other half, of rough bare planking. Its walls are typical of the whole, covered half with the great cooperative effort of the Tuscan School, half with hangings incredibly faded and shabby." Not even Michelangelo's work was exempt from Fuller's severe appraisal. "The great Last Judgment," concluded Fuller, "is typical of the whole: the highest flight of the intellect of the Renaissance obscured by years of careless candle smoke and degraded by the proximity of the rude and clumsy properties left over from the last *funzione* or *festa*."

Fuller's criticism, however, sweeping and severe as it often was, never blinded him to the magnificence of Rome. It was, as he wrote, "inexhaustible" (January 11, 1880). Asked to choose between Chicago and Rome in 1880, Fuller would have unhesitatingly favored Rome. It was a museum, not so much of art as of civilization. It had not one past but many pasts, layer on layer, side by side. More than anything else, the juxtaposition of Rome's many pasts with the present challenged Fuller's imagination while he was there and lived in his memory long after he had left.

Very likely, when Fuller left Rome, he could not have said precisely what his total experience had meant to him. He had come to see objects of art; but, the longer he remained, the greater became his awareness that behind art stands the artist, that people make civilizations, and that the past is most valuable when it renders service to the present. Slowly, yet forcefully, Fuller's attention was being turned away from art toward man in society: civilization in the broadest sense. By the time he left Rome, Fuller was beginning to look at the city with the eye of a novelist.

Although Fuller felt most strongly the intellectual appeal of Rome, he was also emotionally drawn to the city. Occasionally, there were moments when the physical beauty of the city, especially if reinforced by associations with the past, seemed almost overwhelming. This romantic side of Fuller appears with increasing frequency in his notebook as his tour of Rome draws to a close. On January 8, 1880, for example, Fuller ascended the belfry of the church of Saint Saba, and later in the evening he tried to describe what he had seen:

It was within half an hour of sunset. Toward the right, the great mass of the Coliseum caught the ethereal glow which belongs to such a place and time, and the stupendous masses of ruin on the Palatine, crowded with their groups of cypress trees, gave forth all that latent fire which old Roman brickwork is ever ready to yield up at the touch of the setting sun. Off to the left, appeared the wide reaches of the Campagna, flooded and transfigured by the level beams of the fast-sinking sun: I saw the shimmerings of the distant Tiber, the glittering roof of the great basilica of Paolo fuori, the long line of tombs that hedge in the Appian Way, the vast procession of aqueducts stalking brokenly across the country; and bounding all, the beautiful Alban Mountains enveloped in the same, soft, purple haze that diffused itself over the entire prospect—those hills that, in their extreme sensitiveness to the effects of the morning light, nightly pass through chameleon-like a half-score of shades of violet and deepening purples, until the gathering gloom confounds them, all else with the blackness of the already darkened Campagna.

The sun sank lower and I descended to the church itself. In its cool and dusky interior frescoes of long-forgotten saints were crumbling bit by bit from the damp-oozing walls; here and there scraps of scanty mosaics yet maintained their places by an uncertain tenure; the lovely ancient pavement of Opus Alexandrinum was strewn with trampled branches of bay and ilex. . . . In one dark corner a solitary student devoutly knelt in prayer, while from without, in place of the rollicking song which had celebrated but a moment before and with national vigor and heartiness the pleasures of the "speise-saal" now come softly in the subdued tones of some grand Lutheran choral, with a perfect blending of tenors and basses and all the reverential spirit of German devotion.

This passage, flawed as it is by occasionally strained effects and self-conscious alliteration, represents Fuller's early efforts to forge a literary style that would convey the charm and beauty that he felt in Italy.

V   Northern Italy

When Fuller left Rome on March 8, 1880, only two months remained in which to complete his Italian tour. With no abatement in his zeal for sightseeing, he travelled north toward Switzerland, passing through Assisi, Perugia, Florence, Bologna, Ravenna, Ferrara, Venice, Padua, Brescia, Verona, and Milan. Although with the exception of Florence, where he spent a week, and Venice, which occupied him for eighteen days, Fuller spent only two or three days in each of these Italian towns, he found them as delightful and rewarding as any others he had visited.

The entries which Fuller made in his notebook as he journeyed north from Rome reveal the increasing maturity of his critical judgments and foreshadow the principles which he later followed in his writing. Even then, his primary interest focused upon the architectural monuments which lay before him; but his comments, with very little change in emphasis, could apply equally well to the writing of literature. "Beautiful Assisi" Fuller admired extravagantly, particularly for its "air of honest reality" which he found evident in "even the plainest and most prosaic of its structures" (March 8, 1880). He liked the church-fronts which dated from the earliest times of the Tuscan Gothic because they combined "all the beauties of form and color, with a clearness, directness and simplicity not to be too much commended and enjoyed." These are the qualities which Fuller later strived to attain in his writing.

At Perugia, Fuller acknowledged his interest in Etruscan antiquities. From time to time in his notebook Fuller had briefly mentioned Etruscan art objects he had seen in the Vatican and elsewhere in Rome, but now he had an opportunity to visit the chief of the Etruscan antiquities: the great tomb of the Volumni, a few miles from Perugia on the road to Assisi. He later made use of this experience in the opening chapter of *The Chevalier of Pensieri-Vani*. What Fuller admired most about Etruscan art was its honesty and simplicity.

At Florence, Fuller went over the ground he had covered earlier, though he examined for the first time the Campanile. "I was pleased," wrote Fuller in his journal, "to find the workmanship of the Campanile most honest, thorough, and finished.

. . . The Campanile was built on thoroughly medieval principles; Giotto did not give the best he could for the money, but his absolute best" (March 18, 1880). Once more Fuller applied his own principles to what he saw, for, throughout his literary career, he was never content to give less than his "absolute best."

Despite the bad weather which hampered his activities, Fuller managed to enjoy most of the attractions of Venice. "I climbed the Campanile," wrote Fuller in his notebook on March 24, the day after he arrived, "and saw the sun set over a vast and far-reaching aggregation of mud-banks. This evening I took a gondola-ride by full moon through the greater part of the Canalazzo and back through the Guidecca. The occasion, to tell the truth, was beautiful—solemn—tedious—, then, almost doleful." Sharply contrasting with this verdict is the account which Fuller made two days later in his notebook:

> This evening I made a second moonlight excursion on the Grand Canal, and in the vicinity of the Rialto came upon a little festa or something of the sort, where music, lanterns and limelights attracted quite an assembly of gondolas, and made an occasion which I, as a new arrival bursting with poetry and romance, found peculiarly apropos. I took care not to ask what the precise nature of the manifestation was, and kept my gondolier a little removed from the general crowd; so whatever poetry and romance there may have been in a number of gondolas decked out with Chinese lanterns, in the Rialto illuminated by colored lights, and in the singing of several little choruses of male voices, was not sacrificed by the familiarity that breeds contempt.

Despite his ever increasing fastidiousness, apparent in both accounts of his ventures along the canal in moonlight, Fuller derived enjoyment and a large measure of esthetic satisfaction from the palaces, churches, museums, and galleries of Venice.

In Venice, Fuller continued to be concerned with problems of art. "I'm afraid I'm fearfully numb and insensible as regards painting," wrote Fuller in his journal entry for March 30.[4] In dealing with architecture, however, Fuller felt confident of his judgments. After viewing workmen engaged in restoring the "never-failing St. Mark's," Fuller voiced a principle that he would later apply to his own writing:

> The new work is certainly no newer and fresher than the old work which it replaces once was; while, if it is more exact and

accurate, being done by measure instead of by the eye, where is the loss? The loss . . . is largely in the sacrifice of the time-wrought tints and softened *nuances* of the original stones. But these tints and *nuances* and all the rest are quite non-essential, the thought of the architect is the chief consideration. He neither devised nor foresaw the effects that would be wrought by time and weather upon his work; but it is pretty certain that he had a pretty clear notion of what he wanted to do,—of sizes, shapes, colors, masses,—all positive, definable things. What harm in violating mere material, if the idea remain intact? A man's thought *is* his thought, whether expressed in one set of stones or another (April 5, 1880).

Fuller was becoming increasingly aware that "one set of stones" could just as easily be words as marble and that many of the basic principles which were valid in one of these art forms could be made to apply with equal force to the other. For example, while praising the Milan Cathedral only ten days after his comments about the restoration of St. Mark's, Fuller wrote in his journal: "A language should agree only with itself; the same with 'style.' It is possible for even a dialect to be better than the parent language, absolutely speaking; and the union of big architectural influences may produce a style equal to or preferable to that produced by either alone" (April 17, 1880). With Fuller, the most important principle was style, by which he meant the governing concept or forming structure of a work of art. By comparison, the surface details or nuances mattered little, especially if the basic idea or style were clearly discernible. Style, he thought, gave a work of art that "air of honest reality" which for Fuller became the criterion of great art. From this standpoint, Fuller's dislike of the baroque is consistent with his critical principles.

VI Switzerland

After visiting Padua, Verona,[5] Milan, and the Italian lake region, Fuller crossed the border to Switzerland. Although he found the Swiss towns clean, neat, and orderly; the people wholesome and self-respecting; and the scenery everywhere magnificent, Fuller could scarcely hide the fact that, after Italy, Switzerland—or, for that matter, any other country—was an anticlimax. Typical of the comments in his notebook is an entry which he made on May 14, 1880, at Lausanne: "Most of these Swiss towns have no particular sights to see: after six months of Italian churches and museums what a blessed relief and gratification it is to reach a country where all you have to do is to admire the situation of the towns and take a few views over the region round about." Geneva, Berne, Interlachen, Lucerne, and Constance, Fuller found agreeable places for relaxation; but there was not a great deal, except the mountains and the lakes, about which to write; and the city-born Fuller soon tired of trying to describe the scenery.

The first two weeks of June, Fuller spent in Augsburg and Munich. Once more there were cathedrals, churches, museums, and government buildings for him to inspect; but, on the whole, he was disappointed. In Munich, he deplored the Italian influence which he felt pervaded both architecture and painting. "I counted so much," he wrote on June 14 in his journal, "on architectural Munich, and I am disappointed indeed." He objected strenuously to German efforts to imitate the Italian masters of earlier centuries instead of expressing the spirit and ideas of contemporary times.

For Fuller, Oberammergau and Nürnberg were the high points of his tour of Germany. At Oberammergau, he was greatly impressed by the Passion Play, especially by the work of the actors, who, he believed, demonstrated what could be achieved by amateurs. He wrote in his journal:

> The performance and the performers. Both were little short of the marvelous. . . . The actors are peasants. . . . But peasants or whatnot, they are all members of a simple little community shut out from all the world. . . . From the start one finds it well nigh impossible to regard these woodcarving bauers as other than actors in regular standing, of wide experience and high training, who have wholly mastered the art of concealing their art. Such of course they are not and cannot be. If their art be art at all, it is the art that lies so close to nature as to hardly be distinguished from it. Their art, in its broadness, simplicity and sincerity, it pleases me to fancy as resembling the art of the Elizabethan drama; both from and of the people, the race,—twined with their life and their life with it (June 20, 1880).

Thus, the Passion Play at Oberammergau, in Fuller's opinion, represented a practical illustration of the manner in which genuine art could arise out of community life.

The remainder of Fuller's Grand Tour did not perceptibly alter any of his artistic principles. He maintained his thorough program of sightseeing at Stuttgart, Baden-Baden, Strassburg, Heidelberg, Coblentz, and Cologne before reaching Amsterdam on July 10. After a month in Holland he hastened to England to undertake another survey of English cathedrals. On August 19, 1880, Fuller sailed for home; he had been gone almost exactly a year to the day.

When Fuller returned to Chicago, he had already lived through the most important year of his life. Europe had done more to him than he would have cared to admit. In many ways, it had not so much altered him as subtly intensified and, to a degree, hardened traits which had been present, even if latent, in his personality since his experiences at the Allison Classical Academy. In Europe Fuller's compulsive desire for privacy first began to reach the point where privacy became secrecy. In Europe the earliest signs of his obsession with small sums of money became noticeable; and in Europe Fuller's fastidiousness, both in his attitude toward art and in his personal life, became an apparent characteristic.

Much less subtle were the changes which the Old World had wrought in Fuller's outlook. After a year of sightseeing among the art treasures of Europe, Fuller returned to Chicago wholly unfitted, by temperament or by ambition, for a position in Ovington's or in his father's bank, or in any other Chicago business firm. He hated everything associated with business— the routine, the regular working hours, the race for money, and the false standards of value. Most of all, Fuller hated what seemed to him the businessman's confusion of the means with the ends of living.

Fuller had gone abroad to study civilization. He found there not one civilization but monuments of many civilizations side by side with the cultures of the present. For Fuller, the art form by which he could best understand Europe was architecture; but architecture inevitably led him back to the architect—and the architect, in turn, led him to people. After months of sightseeing, Fuller concluded that the artist and the people whose ideas and feelings the artist expressed were just as important as the work of art itself. This idea, which he had vaguely felt in Italy, Fuller was not to define sharply until after he had seen the Passion Play at Oberammergau. Later it became one of the keystones in his theory of art.

Despite his interest in architecture, Fuller never seriously considered becoming an architect. During the year in Europe, he had written criticism of cathedrals, churches, palaces, and public buildings in terms which would apply equally well to writing as to architecture. Writing, which had always been his major interest, continued to occupy his time; and when he returned from Europe, he brought back with him a manuscript of more than four hundred pages which, if not publishable exactly as it was, would at least serve as material for something better to follow. In effect, he had already committed himself to writing.

CHAPTER *3*

Howells or James?

In the eyes of most Chicagoans during the 1880's, Fuller's start toward a career would have seemed very unpromising. In his twenties, a young man could be expected to make progress in some chosen business or profession and to marry. Far from having ambitions for financial success, Fuller seemed to prefer unemployment to a steady job; and he refused the advantages which his family could have given him. To the outward observer, Fuller looked very much like an indolent young man who dabbled occasionally, but without much success, in fiction, poetry, music, and literary criticism. In short, Fuller appeared to be a youthful dilettante whom Europe had ruined for a successful career as a respectable citizen of Chicago.

I The Deficiencies of Home

Fuller's European experience had done much to alienate him from Chicago. During the year abroad, he had been absorbed in architecture, sculpture, painting, music, and writing. In Chicago, there was virtually nothing for the person whose primary interests lay in these fields. Those who "counted" in Chicago talked only about buying, selling, stocks, bonds, real estate, railroads, and meat packing. Fuller looked at his own city and found it ugly, crude, and provincial. As he said, Chicago was engrossed in "non-essentials, empty, earth-bound, low."[1] What had it to offer the shy, sensitive, idealistic Fuller?

The artistic barrenness of the city accentuated his loneliness. He had known loneliness in Europe, but the activity of sightseeing and the knowledge that all around him there were others who shared his devotion to art helped to brighten his outlook. At home, in the absence of esthetic attractions, he felt all the more strongly a want of acquaintances with whom he could talk about the subjects most in his thoughts. After the beginning of the "upward movement" in the 1890's, Fuller found congenial friends among the circle of the Little Room; but, throughout the 1880's, he felt lonely, isolated, and trapped in a city that seemed to have ignored art in the past and would continue to ignore it in the future.

Shortly after his return to the city, Fuller expressed his loneliness and dissatisfaction in his poem "Pensieri Privati." After attacking the city for its drabness, the lack of attention to art, and the emptiness of the mad pursuit of money, Fuller wrote about his longing to return to the Continent where he might "see and hear the best of all the good."[2] Although the two themes were to occupy Fuller's thoughts during the remainder of his life, they were particularly important to him in the decade of the 1880's. Whenever he felt himself defeated and frustrated by Chicago, Fuller romanticized Europe, especially Italy, into a place of fulfillment where the good life could be lived and the crass standards of Chicago did not apply. First and last, Europe was Fuller's refuge. At least, so long as he lived in Chicago, Europe would not fail him.

In April, 1883, Fuller returned to Europe. His itinerary was much the same as it had been three years earlier. After touring the English cathedral towns of Winchester, Salisbury, and Wells, he spent several days in London before crossing to France. He spent two days in Paris, hastened through Switzerland, and stopped briefly at Milan, Genoa, and Pisa. By May 1, he was in Rome.

The fragments which have survived from Fuller's notebook for this tour contrast sharply with the journal he kept in 1879-80.[3] He no longer wrote an account of each day's activities; instead, he planned a series of essays about his travels in which chronology became subordinate to subject matter. The account of his tour of Winchester, Salisbury, and Wells, for example, covers five days of travel; and his description of his journey from London to Rome deals with a two-week period. Instead of merely recounting a mass of details, as he had done earlier, Fuller handled large blocks of material. His literary style has improved, and his comments resemble less and less the facile generalizations of guidebooks.

Throughout his first European trip, Fuller had retained most of his initial enthusiasm. When he returned in September, 1883, from his second European venture, undertaken out of a desperate need to flee the philistinism of Chicago, he had already begun to face the sobering thought that Europe, after all, might not satisfy as a permanent place of residence. Even on his first trip, he had made comparisons, not always to the disadvantage of his own country. Now that he had had the second look, he was even less certain that given a choice—and he knew that sooner or later he would have the financial resources to make a choice—he would take Europe.

II   Literary Beginnings in Boston

For the present, Fuller chose to live in Boston. Earlier, in several stanzas that appear to have been added to "Pensieri Privati," Fuller had suggested that Boston seemed a city combining the Old World and the New and forming a stepping stone between them. Even more, Fuller may have been influenced by the fact that Boston was a center of publishing houses and the home of William Dean Howells. For a young man interested in becoming a writer, Boston had more to offer than Chicago. Fuller took a room at 51 Hancock Street and began to write.

In view of the travel material that he already had in his journals, Fuller's efforts to write humorous pieces seem strange. A book of travel sketches, along the lines of William Dean Howells' *Venetian Life,* would have been a much more likely beginning; but, if Fuller even attempted such a volume, he was unsuccessful. Between January and June, 1884, John Ames Mitchell's recently founded *Life* accepted four pieces from Fuller signed either "B.F." or "Blake Fuller." Although these contributions lack any permanent literary value, they reveal how closely Fuller was keeping up with the current literary situation and subjects which he considered appropriate for writing. The first is a rather ambitious effort at parody having the imposing title: "A Transcontinental Episode, or, Metamorphoses at Muggins' Misery: A Co-operative Novel. By Bret James and Henry Harte."[4] The burlesque of Bret Harte's subject matter and characters' names, together with James's literary style, is mildly amusing. Fuller followed it with a short poem, or song, entitled "Some Day,"⁵ in which he turned the conventional theme of longing for marriage into longing for divorce. Faintly reminiscent of Bret Harte's "Mrs. Judge Jenkins," itself a "sequel" to Whittier's "Maud Muller," Fuller's poem concludes with the line "you pleased me once, but tire me now." Evidently, Fuller objected strongly to the romantic elements in Bret Harte's work.

For his third effort, Fuller returned to the prose parody and again used an impressive title: "The Story of Naptha: A Tale of Culture, Fashion and Duplicity. By Elizabeth Hodgson Phelps and Frances Stuart Burnett."⁶ Readers of *Life* doubtless enjoyed recognizing Fuller's satirical thrusts at the pious sentimentality of the newly published *Beyond the Gates* and the earlier *The Gates Ajar* (1868) by Elizabeth Stuart Phelps (Ward) and his hits at feminine high-society life in Washington depicted by Frances Hodgson Burnett in *Through One Administration* published within the past year. Fuller's final contribution to *Life* was a brief humorous sketch, entitled "The Long and the Short of It. A New England Idyl."⁷ In this piece, he suggested that in the rivalry for a young lady's hand, the youth who can write legibly has the advantage over a rival whose shorthand cannot be deciphered.

Early in the summer of 1884, Fuller submitted two examples of his humorous verse to Henry C. Bunner, editor of *Puck*. Although Bunner responded with words of encouragement, he declined to use either Fuller's "The Ballade of the Bank-Teller" or his "The Ballade of the Touriste."

Although the half-dozen brief satirical pieces by Fuller seem inconsequential beside his later work, they possess an importance as evidence of Fuller's growing appreciation of William Dean Howells and his increasing attention to the meaning of Henry James's European experiences. Fuller, who had walked to "4 Louisburg Square" to stand outside Howells' house for a "curbstone view" and who had felt rewarded when the master "favored the young pilgrim loitering there with a black and forbidding frown,"⁸ had already allied himself with Howells. Fuller's satire on the sentimentality, improbability, and affectation in the fiction of Elizabeth Stuart Phelps and Frances Hodgson Burnett was in accord with Howells' principles. Less than a year later, Howells, himself, was to write something similar in the "Tears Idle Tears" and "Slop, Silly Slop" passages of *The Rise of Silas Lapham.*

The disturbing factor for Fuller was Henry James, the expatriate. Fuller saw that Howells and James, like himself, had felt the attraction of Europe and responded to it in opposite ways. They dramatized the question facing Fuller. Howells had returned to America to write about American subjects, the same general kind of material that Fuller was already using for *Life* and *Puck.* James had chosen to remain abroad and complained that America lacked the materials of fiction. Had Fuller's second European experience been wholly satisfying, he might have made a definite commitment to Europe and sided with Henry James. As it was, James represented a position that Fuller was as yet prepared neither to affirm nor to deny; but the issues were clear-cut, and Fuller returned to Chicago in the summer of 1884 with the problem very much on his mind.

III   Howells or James?

Circumstances more than inclination forced Fuller back to Chicago and kept him there. His father was ill, dying of an undiagnosed disease; and his mother, an invalid, was scarcely able to manage affairs both at the home and at the office. Even though he had little in common with his parents, Fuller would neither refuse help nor shirk what he considered his duty. Early in 1885, George Fuller died, leaving a tangled estate consisting largely of debts and small rental properties. From a sense of obligation, Henry Blake Fuller undertook the management of these properties, which for years represented a source of vexation, worry, and trouble. Although they did not require all of his time, they interfered with his writing and effectively kept him in Chicago until he had almost lost the desire to leave.

In Chicago, Fuller continued his efforts to write. Early in the fall of 1884, the Chicago *Tribune* published his humorous sketch, "The Romance of a Middle-Aged Merchant and His Female Private Secretary."[9] In subject matter and in technique, the story is similar to those he had written in Boston; but its locale is distinctly Chicago. Fuller had not forgotten Howells, nor had he, as his next story demonstrated, forgotten Henry James.

"Pasquale's Picture," written early in 1885 and published in the Chicago *Current,* is Fuller's first successful short story.[10] For it he skillfully constructed a symmetrical plot about a Venetian mother's grief for her son, Pasquale, a gondolier. In the story, an English tourist takes a photograph of Pasquale but fails to develop it properly. A short time later, Pasquale drowns when his gondola overturns. His mother, "old Assunta," consoles herself with the picture; but when the likeness rapidly fades beyond recognition, she becomes heartbroken over having thus twice lost her son. Despite the sentimentality of the characters, the abundance of realistic detail helps to give the story an appearance of plausibility.

The choice of Venice for the setting of "Pasquale's Picture" emphasizes Fuller's uncertainties about the kind of fiction he wished to write and the kind of life he desired to live. In Boston, he had indicated his admiration for Howells' theories of fiction and had scoffed at Henry James's foreign settings and foreign phrases; but Fuller had not yet committed himself to Chicago or, in a wider sense, to America. Howells could be comfortable in Boston, and he had made his decision in favor of America. Fuller was still undecided, and in 1884 and 1885 Europe seemed far more attractive to him than Chicago. Emotionally, Fuller was drawn to Europe and to a way of life symbolized by Henry James, but, intellectually, Fuller admitted the soundness of Howells' position. This dilemma forms the background of Fuller's important essay, "Howells or James?" which he wrote in 1885 but never published.[11]

Fuller began his essay by objecting to the bracketing of William Dean Howells and Henry James in the widely used but, to Fuller, misleading phrase "Howells and James." Fuller contended that, because of the crucial differences between these two novelists, the more accurate and descriptive phrase would be "Howells or James?" Fuller viewed James as an idealist whose approach to fiction was radically different from the realism of Howells. After establishing this thesis, Fuller proposed to ask "which of these two representative writers is to be pronounced most instrumental in the shaping of American fiction?"

Fuller's answer was that Howells, not James, should be acknowledged as the leader of American fiction.

Fuller's essay was partly a response to two articles by Howells in *The Century Magazine*. In "Henry James, Jr." published in 1882, Howells had praised James as the leader of the new school of fiction and had concluded that "it is he who is shaping and directing American fiction."[12] In August, 1884, just a few months before Fuller wrote his article, Howells, reviewing E. W. Howe's novel, *The Story of a Country Town*, and Edward Bellamy's romance, *Miss Ludington's Sister*, had found in them evidence "of the prevalence of realism in the artistic atmosphere" and had asserted that "Mr. Bellamy shows us that the fancy does not play less freely over our democratic levels than the picturesque inequalities of other civilizations."[13] For Fuller, however, Howells' most important statement was that "both books enforce once more the fact that, whatever their comparative value may be, our own things are the best things for us to write of." Although Fuller refrained from making a blunt statement in his essay, his argument shows clearly that he felt James's work was at sharp variance from Howells' statements.

In addition to Howells' articles, the serialization of *The Rise of Silas Lapham*, beginning in *The Century Magazine* in November, 1884, and the appearance, a year earlier, of the fourteen-volume Macmillan edition of James's works made Fuller's appraisal of the two men relevant to current literary production and provided a background for his observations. He believed that he had only to make a "direct comparison" between the two novelists to demonstrate that "Howells is a realist, and James an idealist." In defining James as an idealist, Fuller noted that a man should be judged "by the nature of that whose representation is to him most congenial and self-satisfying." On this basis, asserted Fuller, if James's "most finished and elaborate portraits of persons are marked with exceptional attributes of wit, polish, beauty, culture, wealth, intellect,—and if his most careful and ambitious portraits of places . . . result, after his own peculiar process of selection, rejection, and combination, in a whole of unblemished picturesqueness and unbroken harmony, his claim to the title of idealist seems placed beyond dispute." Even though James "deals, ultimately, in realities," Fuller concluded, "a realism made up of select actualities is pretty apt to come out ideal-istically in the end."

Fuller remarked that realism, as practiced by Howells, "seems coincident with modern democracy." Howells' realism was concerned with "plain every day people and plain every day happiness." By contrast, James appeared interested in the "cul-tivation of the mere top-dressing," those who lived in fortunate circumstances amid the culture of a refined society. Having a "healthy liking for the honest clay and gravel of the great middle stratum," Howells could deal with the "normal earning of money at home"; but James preferred "to deal with the excep-tional and privileged spending of money abroad." Toward virtually every facet of life, Fuller found James's attitude the reverse of Howells'.

The crucial issue for Fuller was the proper subject material for the novelist. Howells, in his review of the novels by Howe and Bellamy, had unequivocably declared that America was the best subject for American writers. On the other hand, James's preference for Europe was equally evident from his novels and from his essay on Hawthorne.[14] For Fuller, this matter was of the highest personal importance because he realized that he, himself, faced these same alternatives. "The time is not far back," wrote Fuller, "when both Howells and James were stationed at the far end of that transatlantic bridge which it is the chief boast and distinction of the latter to have constructed between the Old World and the New. Howells, with a clear perception of the direction in which the cat . . . was about to jump, crossed over a few years back . . . and has stead-fastly remained with us ever since." James had remained in Europe and had written about Europe.

In 1885, Fuller was trying to decide whether to follow Howells or James. He realized that the cat had jumped to America and that "the writer who is most thoroughly permeated with the realistic spirit may confidently expect the widest hearing and the securest place." Yet Fuller had never liked "plain every day people," and nothing could have been less interesting to him than the prospect of writing about the "normal earning of money" in Chicago. Howells, it seemed to Fuller, was prob-ably right, but Fuller would neither concede the point nor publish his essay.

IV   The Chevalier

The writing of "Howells or James?" failed to settle the
issues for Fuller. He envied Howells, who, apparently, had
been able to put Italy out of mind and to accept Boston. For
Fuller, as he fretted over repairs to the furnaces, plumbing, and
roofing of his mother's apartments, Italy remained the center
of his intellectual life. To him, Italy was a living presence, the
source of both his pleasure and his dissatisfaction, and a constant standard by which he measured Chicago. However cogent
the arguments in favor of Howells' position might be, Fuller
could not put aside his longing for Italy.

In 1886, Fuller was working in a small business office on
Lake Street, one of the busiest areas in Chicago. For him, as
he said, it was a time of "considerable discomfort and depression"[15] To relieve his tension—Fuller said "largely for my
own entertainment and consolation"—and without thought
of publication, he began to write *The Chevalier of Pensieri-Vani*
on the back of an envelope taken out of the wastebasket. "It was
started," said Fuller, "to make good certain omissions in my
European experiences, and was designed, in the first instance,
to describe places that I neglected to visit, when 'on the
ground.' "[16] Fuller did not restrict himself to places he had
never seen. "Of course," he continued, "I have been to Pisa and
Ravenna and Orvieto, and even to San Gimignano, (some
of them more than once); but Viterbo and Pienza and Anagni
and many others are among the pensieri-vani—the unavailing
after thoughts."

Despite his saturation with "things Italian," Fuller found
the composition of his book difficult. He wrote slowly, polishing
his sentences carefully, inventing incidents as he went along.
He felt no compulsion for haste, yet he found the work dom-
inating his thoughts as he worked in the office, as he ate his
meals in downtown restaurants and oyster houses, or as he
walked along the sidewalks of Chicago. He recorded his slow
advance, chapter by chapter, in a small pocket memorandum-
book. Early in 1887 he had finished, and he decided to publish
the manuscript.

"For a year or two," wrote Fuller to the literary editor of
the Boston *Transcript,* the manuscript "knocked around from

pillar to post, and then, for two or three more, it lay forgotten in a trunk. It was declined by most of the best known houses of New York, Boston, and Philadelphia; one luminous and historic firm in New York read the manuscript, quoted me cost of manufacture, and then refused to publish the book, at my expense."[17] In 1890, however, the J. G. Cupples Company of Boston agreed to publish the volume at Fuller's expense; and late in November the firm deposited for copyright *The Chevalier of Pensieri-Vani together with Frequent References to the Prorege of Arcopia. By Stanton Page.* Shortly afterwards, the slight volume, priced at fifty cents in paper and one dollar in cloth, was placed on sale in Boston. It was, as Harriet Monroe later remembered, a "cheaply made, badly printed first edition,"[18] in no way indicative of the stir that it would make in Boston literary circles or the fame that it would bring the author.

In 1887, however, as Fuller finished writing *The Chevalier of Pensieri-Vani,* he could not have forecast the eventual success of his production. What he had written, Fuller himself recognized, had been fashioned out of his own need to solve the same personal problem which lay in the background of the earlier essay "Howells or James?" Once more Fuller opposed the attractions of leisurely living among the esthetic pleasures of an Italian past to the arid commercialism of modern America. In *The Chevalier of Pensieri-Vani,* Fuller tipped the scales toward James and Italy; and in his pocket memorandum-book Fuller described his work as "idealistic," [19] the same word he had used to characterize the writings of Henry James.

Having taken the position, temporarily at least, in favor of James and the Italian past, Fuller began to compose the libretto, voice, and piano music for two light operas, "Mariquita" and "Pipistrello," set in early seventeenth-century Spain and Italy. For such an inexperienced composer as Fuller, they represented ambitious projects. Fuller had received a reasonably thorough training in piano and organ; he had had experience with choral groups; and he had composed several songs. He also possessed a general familiarity with the history of music and a special knowledge of the music of Mozart and the operettas of Gilbert and Sullivan. But he knew virtually nothing about orchestration, and even the writing of musical notation became for him an enormous labor.

The two operettas, which Fuller never succeeded in getting either produced or published, though he tried repeatedly, have survived in two beautifully written manuscripts. To a very marked degree, they are patterned after the work of Gilbert and Sullivan which Fuller admired extravagantly. For his operettas, Fuller invented ingenious, highly complicated plots turning on mistaken identities which are solved in Gilbert and Sullivan fashion. The lyrics and music occasionally exhibit a sparkle which approaches the level of his masters, but the best feature of these works is the occasional flash of satirical humor which brings character and song to life.

In his sketches for *Life* and *Puck,* Fuller had already shown that he had a keen sense of humor and knew how to make a telling point in satire. With the example of Gilbert and Sullivan's thrusts at contemporary issues before him and with his awareness of Howells' insistence upon the importance of American subjects to American writers, Fuller's choice of European characters and European historical settings for his operettas may only be understood in terms of the same commitment to Italy that lay behind *The Chevalier of Pensieri-Vani.* Had he selected the targets for his satire from issues relevant to American life, he might have been far more successful than he was. The producers and directors of American musical comedies were not interested in Fuller's Spanish or Italian pieces. The months of painstaking labor that Fuller devoted to them represented wasted effort from which he could salvage nothing except the knowledge that he was not a composer.

CHAPTER 4

The Chevalier and the Chatelaine

A lthough by 1890 the phenomenal success of such roman-
cers as F. Marion Crawford had convincingly demonstrated
the fascination that Italian romance held for American readers,
the public for *The Chevalier of Pensieri-Vani* was limited. Fuller's book was not everybody's book. For those who had travelled
leisurely in Italy, felt the peculiar charm of its countryside,
known the temptation to linger, and then made the decision
to return to America, the volume had a distinctive, nostalgic
appeal. Especially to the generation before Fuller, the earlier
travellers like Charles Eliot Norton, James Russell Lowell, and
even William Dean Howells, who had gone to Italy in the 1850's
and 1860's, the Chevalier spoke as an old friend. Like Fuller,
they had been "on the ground," and, like him, they also had
their own particular *pensieri-vani*. For them and for those, including the "old settlers," who already found themselves unable
to keep up with the ever accelerating pace of life in the cities,
Fuller's book had relevance. These readers constituted not a
large audience but certainly an influential one.

I   The Reception of *The Chevalier of Pensieri-Vani*

Fuller's book might have gone entirely unnoticed if a copy
had not been sent to Charles Eliot Norton a few days after
the first edition was placed on sale at Boston's Old Corner
Bookstore. Norton, widely known as an authority on Dante
and a lover of Italy, immediately acclaimed the book as a work
of genius and wrote to the unknown author to express the
"exquisite pleasure" which he had received from *The Chevalier
of Pensieri-Vani*.[1] Norton then sent a copy to James Russell
Lowell as a Christmas gift. After reading it, Lowell, then near
the end of his career and considered by many persons the most

cultured man in America, praised the work highly and also wrote to Fuller to express admiration.[2] What impressed both Norton and Lowell was Fuller's ability to render the charm of the Italian landscape in a highly polished prose. Fuller could not have found two more distinguished or influential sponsors for his first book.

With Norton and Lowell enthusiastic admirers, *The Chevalier of Pensieri-Vani* was assured at least a measure of success. By February 12, 1891, when a lengthy review appeared in the Boston *Transcript*, the book was already being widely discussed. The reviewer pointed out that "Professor Norton introduced this delightful Italian to his friends; they, of course, to other friends, and so he goes on from house to house with his wit and his charm and his elegance." What astonished the writer for the *Transcript*, however, was the identity of the author:

> After having taken all the credit possible for the growing love that Cambridge and Boston have for the Chevalier Pensieri-Vani, we hesitate to say that "Stanton Page" is a Chicago man, and a young man, by name Henry Fuller. It was such writing as this our elder writers gave us in their youthful days, yet here is no touch of youth in the finished style, in the sunny humor, in the quality, quality, quality! Yet it will not do too much to begrudge him to the proud commercial city of the West. Probably he has a grandfather—with this leisure of enjoyment in his Italian wanderings. And if he has a grandfather, ten to one that he is proud that he came from Massachusetts.

Later reviewers of *The Chevalier of Pensieri-Vani* were not so kind as the *Transcript* had been in suggesting a relationship between Fuller's book and his native Chicago. Eastern papers frequently expressed great surprise that anything artistic could come "out of Chicago—out of that most Godless, lawless, metropolitan, democratic Nazareth."[3] The Boston *Gazette* observed that "were one to rank things on a scale of ten, the scholarship of Chicago would be marked two, the polish of Chicago, one, and the historical sense of Chicago somewhere about minus fifteen." But it concluded that Fuller's book would make him "famous everywhere, except in Chicago. There is nothing in Chicago so unlike Chicago as 'The Chevalier of Pensieri-Vani.'"[4] Such remarks were met by the Chicago press, particularly the Chicago *Evening Post,* with loud praise for Chicago and, incidentally, Fuller's book.

Although the newspaper controversy may have temporarily helped sales, *The Chevalier of Pensieri-Vani* would have made its way on artistic merits only. Norton and Lowell had actually established its place, but their remarks were seconded by the approval of such admirers as Richard Watson Gilder, F. B. Sanborn, Mrs. Louise Chandler Moulton, and Agnes Repplier, whose review article in *Lippincott's Monthly Magazine* for June, 1891, was widely read. By the end of 1891, the fact that J. G. Cupples and Company had issued three editions indicated the steady, if modest, demand for the book.

In the spring of 1892, Fuller transferred *The Chevalier of Pensieri-Vani* to the Century Company; and, under the direction of Richard Watson Gilder, the firm brought out a new, revised, fourth edition, the first to bear Fuller's name and to include illustrative drawings at the beginning of each chapter. In addition to correcting many of the errors of the earlier editions, Fuller added a dedication to Charles Eliot Norton and a chapter entitled "Siena: A Vain Abasement." This edition, which the Century Company sponsored as if it were a new book, prompted extensive reviews and renewed discussion of Fuller's achievement.

Because of the unqualified recognition accorded *The Chevalier of Pensieri-Vani* by the literati of New England, whose authority in matters of art was still supreme, Henry Blake Fuller emerged as Chicago's leading writer. Coming to prominence, as he did, on the eve of the World's Columbian Exposition, Chicago's dramatic effort to assert to the rest of the nation her cultural, as well as her industrial and scientific, achievements, Fuller seemed to many Chicagoans the literary man of the hour. He proved that Chicago had arrived culturally. He was a native-born product who could meet the Eastern arbiters of culture on their own terms—that those terms were Italian and not Midwestern American mattered not the slightest.

Contemporary reviewers who had not had the Italian experiences of Norton and Lowell "on the ground" found *The Chevalier of Pensieri-Vani* impossible to classify and difficult to evaluate. They agreed that although the volume was clearly a product of genius, it was not a novel, a travel book, an autobiography, or a collection of essays. After reaching Agnes Repplier's conclusion that the book was "equally guileless of plot or purpose, of dramatic incidents or realistic details,"[5] most reviewers praised the work in terms of its exquisite style and "bits of golden fantasy."[6] If there lurked beneath the humor and the gentle satire a serious message, the critics of Boston and Chicago failed to discover it. Had the reviewers seen Fuller's journals for his European trips in 1879 and 1883, or had they read his unpublished essay "Howells or James?" or had they correctly estimated his attitude toward Chicago, they would have understood much more clearly what Fuller was trying to accomplish. The key to the book, hidden to almost all except those whose experiences had paralleled those of Fuller, lay in its relationship to Fuller himself. In a very literal and personal sense, *The Chevalier of Pensieri-Vani* was Fuller's own testament.

Despite Fuller's assertion that his book was designed to describe places in Italy which he had never visited, the entries in his journal during the winter of 1879-80 show plainly that, with only minor exceptions, he was thoroughly familiar with the Italian cities and towns that formed the locale of his book. Pisa, Florence, San Gimignano, Colle, Siena, Orvieto, Rome, and Venice were the places which had meant a great deal to him. In particular, the towns of Tuscany and the rural areas surrounding them Fuller had described again and again in his journal as charming, beautiful, picturesque. Fuller had only to refer to what he had written on the scene to imagine what they would have been "with beaming sky and blooming flowers" (3). The journal thus furnishes the solid basis in fact for the travels of the Chevalier of Pensieri-Vani, and at times the correspondence between the two approaches the level of paraphrase.

II The Chevalier's Adventures

Although *The Chevalier of Pensieri-Vani* derives a measure of unity from the successive appearances of the titular hero and, less frequently, of the subordinate characters, from the evenness of Fuller's style, and, most importantly, from thematic relationships, the series of incidents which constitute the plot are only loosely connected to one another. Indeed, each episode in the adventures of the Chevalier stands by itself, making a separate, satirical, and humorous "point." The chapter titles, all of which begin with a place name, indicate the locale of the incident to be related. As the book opens, the Chevalier of Pensieri-Vani, a poor young gentleman, "who loved the post-roads of Tuscany . . . and every antique stone of the fair Italian land," is travelling toward Rome to meet a group of kindred spirits. An authority on Etruscan monuments, he has discovered an Etruscan tomb, entered it, and taken from the Old Etruscan Lucumo upon the bier a crown of burnished gold. The Chevalier wishes only to place the crown upon his head and then return it to its proper place in the tomb, because, Fuller explained, he is "modern and an archaeologist" (6).

After meeting his friends just beyond the castle of Ronciglione, the Chevalier returns to the tomb to replace the crown; but he finds that "the old warrior, after having triumphed for threescore years over the chances of war, and the dangers of fire and flood,—after sleeping calm and undisturbed through the tempests and earthquakes of three thousand years,—had crumbled pitifully away to nothing before the vagrant breezes of a summer day" (9). The Chevalier, who knows he has done an evil deed, has only contempt for himself; and Fuller under-scored the point of the incident:

> The stern old warrior-priest, who might have wakened to a Nero, a Hildebrand, a Torquemada, a Napoleon, had been invited to rest his blinking and startled gaze upon a Garrison, a Nightingale, a Peabody. Slumbering through the long ages wherein might made right, he had been called back to light to participate in an epoch of invertebrate sentimentalism. Drunk on deep draughts of blood and iron, his reviver now sought to force him to munch the dipped toast of a flabby humanitarianism, and to sip the weak tea of brotherly love. This refreshment he had loftily declined.

Never again does the Chevalier attempt to open an Etruscan tomb. The contrast between the past and the present, suggested but not insisted upon, forms a recurrent theme throughout the remainder of the book.

In the next five chapters of *The Chevalier of Pensieri-Vani*, Fuller related an equal number of incidents in the leisurely travels of the Chevalier. At Pisa, he learns to his chagrin that opera audiences in Italian towns "quite refused to be bought up and delivered" (22). The pursuit of an unknown madonna, rumored to have been painted by Perugrino, takes him through many Tuscan towns. At Siena, he encounters the Duke of Avon and Severn; at Orvieto, the Chevalier improvises brilliantly on the cathedral organ; and at Rome, he passes an expert's judgment upon the authenticity of the Iron Pot. In this last episode of the senseless rivalry among diplomats and collectors for a spurious archaeological treasure, Fuller's satire upon those whose approach to the past is either selfishly or commercially inspired reaches its most humorous and effective level.

In the last seven chapters of the book, the Chevalier shares the leading role with his friend, the Prorege of Arcopia. They are together as the Prorege instructs his pupil, George W. Occident, in the advantages of a despotic paternalism over modern democracy; but the Prorege does not accompany the Chevalier to Anagni when he visits the lonely expatriate Gregorianius whose death later sends the Chevalier to Ravenna in search of material to complete this eminent scholar's history of Italian civilizations. At Venice, the Chevalier opposes his knowledge of bibliography to that of the Duke of Avon and Severn in competition for a small collection from the famous Aldine press. The incident concludes aboard the Prorege's yacht when all of the characters gather for a cruise in the Adriatic near the coast of Arcopia.

After the characters have gone their separate ways, the Chevalier recalls "how much he had left unseen, how much undone. How many masterpieces remained unviewed, how many landscapes had been left unsketched, unpainted . . . how many memorable spots he had left unvisited! Such are some of the *pensieri vani* that torment the home-come voyager" (181). To Fuller, as he wrote *The Chevalier of Pensieri-Vani* in Chicago and recalled the pleasures of his Italian tour during the winter of 1879-80, the Chevalier's words possessed a poignant, intensely personal significance.

III   A Band of Expatriates

The characters in *The Chevalier of Pensieri-Vani,* whose allegorical names suggest a quality or principal fact about them, exist primarily as vehicles for Fuller's own opinions. Like many of the characters in the novels of Henry James, they are exceptional persons—aristocratic, talented, and perceptive. Financially, they are all in circumstances which permit them leisure to follow their own wishes; and several, like George W. Occident, are immensely wealthy. With the possible exception of the Prorege of Arcopia, whose land is a combination of Arcadia and Utopia, each of the characters has come to Italy in the belief voiced by Occident that life there will be "better worth living than he could make it seem in the region where he had had the misfortune to be born" (96-97). In one way or another, they are all expatriates. None would have found life tolerable in Chicago.

The titular hero, often referred to simply as the Cavaliere, expresses Fuller's deep attachment to Italy; his preference for the past over the present; his enjoyment of leisure, bachelorhood, and privacy; his interest in architecture; his taste for music; and his appreciation of the charm of a rural landscape— in short, Fuller's vision of the good life. At other times, the Cavaliere voices Fuller's own self-doubts, his apprehension of failure, and his pessimism. As one would expect, Fuller consistently treated the Cavaliere seriously and sympathetically. He may be taken as Fuller's effort to suggest a mean between the two extremes represented by two other principal characters, the Prorege of Arcopia and George W. Occident.

As viceroy of a small Adriatic kingdom, the Prorege espouses the advantages of a despotic, paternalistic form of government, the antithesis of democracy. In the strictly ordered, despotic government of the Prorege, the arts of architecture and opera flourish magnificently; and the Prorege considers himself mainly responsible for their promotion. The manner of life in Arcopia suggests the methods by which the arts were encouraged during the greatest periods of artistic achievement in the history of Italy; but, however greatly Fuller may have admired the Prorege's refinement, his ambitions for stimulating artistic creativity in music and architecture, and his cultivated sensitivity to the feelings of others, Fuller could not approve of the selfishness and vanity which seemed the necessary concomitant to the Prorege's otherwise admirable qualities.

For his pupil, the Prorege has taken the wealthy and "promising young barbarian," George W. Occident, who at the age of twenty-two—Fuller's age in 1879 when he first went to Italy— has left his native Shelby County in search of a more meaningful life. In his "uninstructed state," commented Fuller, Occident had "no conception of the significance, social, artistic, historical, which brick and stone may take unto themselves, and he could ramble about the streets of Verona or Siena or Vicenza,— almost every one of them a free gallery of masterpieces,—seeing nothing and quite unconscious that there was anything to see." Occident, however, is "extremely bright," and has "picked up ideas with the utmost readiness." What troubles the Prorege is "the number of points on which the young man's opinions were already completely shaped and tenaciously held" (95-96). Occident's opinions concern the nature of government, the importance of activity for the sake of activity, and the structure of society; and in all these matters Occident maintains the positions which a young man from Chicago might be expected to advance. Thus, Occident becomes the opposite pole from the Prorege. If analogy were needed, Fuller would have argued that Occident's position approached that of Howells, while the Prorege would have been sympathetic to the point of view of Henry James.

The Chevalier, the Prorege, and Occident are ably supported by a cast of minor characters. The most delightful of them is perhaps Hors-Concours, who lives in the Alps of Savoy as the present owner of "the few literal acres of cloud-draped rocks and chestnut-trees" (12) to which the Seigneurs of Hors-Concours, at the end of seven centuries, still cling. Like the Chevalier, Hors-Concours spends most of his time in Italy, shares the Chevalier's views on marriage, and enjoys "like him the life of pleasant and self-indulgent irresponsibility which may be led, up to a certain age, without provoking too severe a condemnation from the more serious and sober-minded section of society" (55). In the final chapter of the book, when Hors-Concours announces his intention of marrying the Princess Altissimi, the Chevalier lapses into a fit of despondency.

The Duke of Avon and Severn, the Contessa Nullaniuna, and the Margravine of Schwahlbach-Schreckenstein, the only characters who have nothing in common with Fuller, are cast in much less sympathetic roles. The Duke, a cold, haughty, snobbish Englishman, plays the villain's role in the incidents involving the Madonna Incognita and the Aldine books. The Contessa, whom Fuller satirized as "a woman of genius whose peculiar gifts—I will tell you some time what they were—had never received their full measure of recognition" (17), successfully gratifies her vanity at the expense of the Prorege only to be humiliated in revenge while a guest aboard the Prorege's yacht. The Margravine, Fuller's portrait of an energetic dowager, enjoys a dubious triumph in the story of the Iron Pot. These characters, although types, are more fully realized by Fuller than the major characters who stand more for ideas than for individuals.

IV The Style Absolute

In *The Chevalier of Pensieri-Vani,* Fuller's style conforms to the concept of the "style absolute" which he had formulated in the notebooks written during his travels in Italy in 1879-80. In effect, Fuller's objective was to develop a style in which there would be a complete harmony between feeling and thinking and a rigid adherence to what he called the "fundamental proprieties" of writing.[7] On the one hand, he knew that he must avoid the flaws of clumsy alliteration, strained effects, and bookish images that marred many of the "purple passages" of his notebooks; and, on the other hand, he must achieve a consistent tone and the proper balance of description, narration, and sentiment.

Almost from the very beginning of the book, Fuller established rapport between himself (as narrator) and the reader by invoking the perennial appeal of the unknown and far away in a series of rhetorical questions that are a feature of his style.

> Dost know the tombs of Castel d'Asso? The towers of San Gimignano? The outlooks from Montepulciano? The palaces of Pienza? The cloisters of Oliveto Maggiore? Hast ever penetrated the obscure renown of the Fanum Voltumnae,—or followed the fading frescoes of the Grotta del Trinclinio,—or studied the lengthening shadows of the Val di Chiana,—or boated it across to the lonely isles of the Lago Trasimeno? No? Nor have I. How Pensieri-Vani would pity us both! For he has; such things are his life (2).

These, and scores of other equally obscure place names with

which Fuller larded his book, could be identified with the help
of a Baedeker, but probably very few persons were willing to
read holding *The Chevalier of Pensieri-Vani* in one hand and
an Italian guidebook in the other.[8] The very obscurity of the
place names serves Fuller's purpose by lending a strange, romantic atmosphere to the book.

The romantic atmosphere of the volume is further intensified by Fuller's repeated use of his own memories of Italian
scenes associated with the Italian past. In effect, he piled the
past upon the past in sentences of extraordinary length whose
content is primarily a series of picture-impressions consisting
of both visual and historical material. Although generally successful, the "style absolute" occasionally threatens, as in the
following passage, to overwhelm the stylist and to try the
patience of even the most leisurely reader.

> When you have made your pilgrimage over these slighted and
> deserted tracts, so frequently ignored by the too hurried gleaner,
> you have gathered in such a harvest of recollections as will render
> the very name of Rome a delight to you long after the thoughts
> of the greater roba di Roma have merged themselves into a mass
> of indistinct memories—recollections of long strolls through sol-
> itary lanes, among whose withered hedgerows the quick lizard
> writhes; of unlawful trespassings on quiet gardens and cloisters,
> enriched with sculptured wells and overshadowed with palm or
> pine; of entrance into some ancient, unchurched church, with its
> half-forgotten treasure of carved altar and mosaic pavement,
> where frescoed saints and angels crumble slowly from the damp
> walls, and where the grim old mosaics of the apse bend down
> upon you and gloomily return your stare; of tutelary saints, whose
> acquaintance you then made, and whose legends you then heard
> for the first time; of monkish ciceroni, who hardly take the trouble
> to conceal their incredulity as they recite their time-honored
> untruths, yet slyly wonder if the inquisitive stranger will be con-
> siderate enough to disguise his own; of weak and withered old
> men who open up their obscure haunts to the infrequent visitor
> and timidly direct his attention to poor little collections of an-
> tiquities—scraps of marble or fragments of sculpture dug from
> the neighboring vineyard or picked up by their own doorsteps
> (70-71).

As the source of Fuller's stylistic effects, the Italian past took
second place only to his boundless admiration for form, visual

form, whether embodied in cathedrals, monasteries, palazzos, mosaics, or the landscape itself. The traces of Fuller's experiences as an indefatigable sightseer appear everywhere in his work; indeed, it is through his descriptions of the Italian landscapes that he best communicates the romantic charm of Italy to his readers. Nowhere does Fuller convey his recollections more effectively or more subtly than in the description of the Prorege at Siena as he walks through the "shrubs and flower-beds of the Lizza toward the *pallone* ground which lay beneath the fortifications of the Fortezza":

He selected a lofty perch in the angle of a convenient bastion,— a position which commanded at once a good view of the grounds below him and of the old town itself sprawled out carelessly beneath and about him. On one of the huddled hills opposite rose the cathedral, with its dome and its bell-tower and its vast skeletonic nave; and on others appeared the façades of churches and the towers of convents, like knots in a loosely tangled skein. In the midst of all this the great tower of the Municipio shot up and blossomed forth, and encompassing all was a long, low heaving of brown and half-denuded hills, set here and there with timeworn monasteries and with villas reached through long avenues of cypresses (49).

At times the peace and quietness of an old church, some broken bits of mosaic, or "the cypressed villas, the ruinous old abbeys in delightful Gothic brickwork, the campanili of village churches rising from the olived slopes of hillsides" (34), bring back to Fuller and to his readers the charm and beauty of Italy. More than anything else the remarkable consistency and evenness of the "style absolute" enabled Fuller to arouse in his readers the same romantic, nostalgic feelings for Italy that he himself felt.

V Meanings

By tacitly ignoring the characters and by praising Fuller's skill in rendering the "charm of Italy," Charles Eliot Norton defined the appeal of *The Chevalier of Pensieri-Vani* for most readers. Fuller had determined precisely what Italy had to give and what Italy demanded in return from the foreign traveller. "The ability to perceive," wrote Fuller, "to understand what one perceives, to extract the full measure of profit and enjoyment by so understanding,—this must be in great part the wealth of a pilgrim in Italy" (57). He could have added, what he took for granted, that for perception on these levels abundant leisure was an essential requisite. Out of his own Italian experiences he concluded that "the Italian civilization addresses itself primarily to the eye, but after, with immense reaches of depth and breadth, to the intellect." The comment accounts for the particular elements Fuller admired in Italy as well as what he failed to include in his portrait. The contributions of Italian civilization to religion, to law, and to literature, except as they related to architecture, Fuller slighted or ignored altogether, both in his extensive accounts of his travels in Italy during the winter of 1879-80 and in *The Chevalier of Pensieri-Vani.*

Fuller emphasized his admiration for Italy and, more particularly, the Italian past, by his criticism of modern times. Old Lucumo, stern Etruscan warrior and ruler, awakens in an age of sentimentality in which he declines, symbolically, to participate. His crown remains "but there was no head on which to place it" (9). In the modern world, there are many men, like Occident, possessed of millions but unable to find any useful end for their activities and utterly ignorant of those things which could make life beautiful or meaningful. By contrast, the historical and artistic monuments of Italy testify to the lives of strong men who "could dare and do, who could will and have" (113). From them, even the Chevalier "shrank away as a very weak, pitiful, forceless creature." Fuller pressed the point:

The stippling technique of his own day seemed immeasurably poor and paltry compared with the broad, free, sketchy touch with which these men dashed off their stirring lives; and he stood abashed before that fiery and robust intensity which, so gloriously indifferent to the subtilties [*sic*] of the grammarian, the niceties of the manicure, and the torments of the supersensitive self-analyst, could fix its intent upon some definite desire and move forward unswervingly to its attainment. Poor moderns! he sighed, who with all our wishing never reached our end, and with all our thinking never know what we really think, after all.

Whatever the Moderns have touched has been blighted. In

the story of the Iron Pot, Fuller attacked those who, lacking any personal enjoyment of art objects from the past, fight for their possession because of their commercial value; by contrast, the Chevalier's modest collection contains items of no great monetary value, yet they afford him lasting pleasure. Fuller's attack upon the desecration wrought by the Moderns reaches a climax in the closing pages of the book. As the Prorege's yacht passes the "once-lovely convent-isle of Sant' Elena," now the site of an iron-foundry, the Prorege averts his eyes: "For Italy, the Modern, the United, had set her heavy official foot upon this little clump of sea-encircled foliage;—no beneficent Minerva whose one light stamp called forth the olive, but brutal Progresso, whose iron-shod hoof had trampled the olive down, together with a hundred other gracious and other tender things, into the muck and mire, and had heaped upon it the hundred revolting forms that refuse may assume" (162-63).

Fuller's sense of outrage reached the greatest intensity as he contemplated the utter disregard and contempt with which the Moderns treat both past and future generations:

> Whose was the earth? our indignant prince would ask himself when considerations of this kind rose up to irritate him. Was it the exclusive possession of those merely who were now living out their brief day upon it, or was it something more—the foothold and heritage of generations yet to come? Who could make good to those of the coming century the felled trees, the gashed and leveled hills, the polluted ponds and choked-up streams that signalized our present dealings with outraged and suffering Mother Nature? Who was to render back to them an earth as beautiful as that which we ourselves received as our right,—an earth whose possession and enjoyment is as much, as inalienably, their right as ours? More; what power could save us—us, full of small greeds and great irreverences—from the amaze and scorn and contempt and indignation of millions yet unborn? (163–64).

The sentiments of the Prorege meet the approval of the Duke of Avon and Severn who has exiled himself from England rather than witness "the last stages of that transformation which had all but changed the most lovely land in the whole world into the most hideous" (165). Both the Duke and the Prorege associate the havoc which the Moderns have wreaked upon the beauty of nature and the past with the advance of democracy;

and, when Occident expatiates upon "the beauties and blessings of popular suffrage" in America, the Prorege declares that self-government on any but a small scale and in a young and simple society is "a ludicrous and hideous fallacy" (166-67). He concludes that "no great city could be self-governing" and that the first desideratum is "a ruler, to save the people from itself."[9] Anyone with a knowledge of the corruption in Chicago's city government during the 1880's would have understood the implications of Fuller's comments.

The Prorege, whose connection with the agrarian Arcopia makes him a useful fictional device for expressing Fuller's ideas, strongly opposes modern industrialism. "Society had never courted failure or bid for misery more ardently," he declares, "than when it had accepted an urban industrialism for a basis" (168). The statement, of course, reflects Fuller's sympathy with the older, rural America whose rapid disappearance he was witnessing in Chicago.

The growth of industrialism, argues the Prorege, makes it "more and more difficult to discriminate between a man and a highly specialized machine," and to support his position, he cites the great "Vashingtone" of Occident's own country. To Occident's reply that Washington was never "considered much of a financier," the Prorege indignantly retorts: "If it were necessary . . . to discriminate between a man and a machine, it was doubly, trebly necessary to discriminate between a man and a mere money-machine" (168-69).

Had Fuller's Chicago critics correctly estimated *The Chevalier of Pensieri-Vani,* they would have known that the hard core of his book is an attack upon modern industrialism, modern bigness, and modern governmental corruption. Without a distinguished past, without concern for nature or beauty, and without any more useful purpose than the acquisition of material goods, life in Chicago, it seemed to Fuller, had little to offer the individual who would not consent to become a "mere money-machine." Admittedly, Italy was not perfect; but it was demonstrably better than Chicago. At least the expatriate in Italy possessed more of the peace, beauty, and dignity of life than the toilers in Chicago's industrial society.

VI   The Expatriate's Life

At Anagni, in the ancient territory of the Volsci and Hernici, the Chevalier of Pensieri-Vani encounters the venerable medievalist Gregorianius, a German expatriate of the generation of 1830. Even when he was a young man, Italy had been the great passion of his life; and, like Fuller himself, Gregorianius, before he had ever visited Italy, had made himself familiar with Italian architecture, history, and painting. During the early years of his career, Gregorianius had buried himself among the medieval monuments of Tuscany. As he became older, he progressed to the study of classical antiquity at Rome; and, having mastered the mysteries of the Forum, he advanced to the even more recondite subject of the Etruscan civilization. At some moment, perhaps imperceptible even to himself, Gregorianius had passed the point when he could have returned to Germany to make a successful career.

Finally, having mastered almost everything known about Italian civilization, he concluded, as an old man, that "nothing short of the Utterly Unknowable could seem an adequately dignifying study." The scene of these final investigations was to be "the hoary cyclopean towns among the Hernican hills, where the venerable and the unintelligible exist in an ideal union" (117); but, before he could make tangible progress in his research, Gregorianius seemed increasingly to turn his attention back to the medievalism of his earlier days. As the Chevalier stood by, Gregorianius lay on a couch, "languidly watching the mountain-sweep of the clouds, and murmuring to himself of many a far-off time and many a bygone name" (119). Here the lonely old expatriate died.

Fuller wished his readers to understand that Gregorianius had finally mastered what the Italian past had to offer, but for his knowledge he had alienated himself from his own native land only to become an alien in a foreign land. He becomes an example of the futility of "living through other lives, and making but a thin blood by dieting on the unnutritious husks of a dead-and-gone past" (113). He becomes a warning both to the Chevalier and to Fuller himself who realized that his own life might possibly end in this fashion. The warning serves no useful purpose for the Chevalier, who, Fuller told his readers, soon appears "to have wholly slipped back into his own ways and to have become too confirmed and too inveterate a 'looker-on' to justify any great hope of his conversion" (119).

VII Personal Implications

Fuller's complaints against the standards of modern urban industrialism are best understood against the background of his own life. Though disguised as the opinions of allegorical figures in a book of "idealistic travel-fiction," the sentiments are those of Fuller. They are, in fact, the passionate protest of a man who felt he was caught in an environment that negated all he thought beautiful, valuable, and enjoyable in living. Viewed rightly, *The Chevalier of Pensieri-Vani* is actually a book about Chicago, although the city is never mentioned by name.

The agony of Fuller was not merely that he longed hopelessly to get away from Chicago and return to Italy. What tormented him most was the specter, the fear, the doubt which, because of his skeptical mind, he could not fail to entertain and which in a lifetime he was never wholly to exorcise—that is, the possibility that for all its charm, beauty, and peace, Italy, for the expatriate, was a dead end, a blind alley. This possibility Fuller would approach only indirectly through the story of Gregorianius, but its application to Fuller's fictional self, the Chevalier, and its parallel to Fuller's own life are strikingly apparent.

In 1886, as Fuller was writing *The Chevalier of Pensieri-Vani*, the choice between the life of an expatriate and that of a citizen of Chicago—between the points of view represented in Fuller's mind by Howells and James—was still for him a live option. He possessed a firm grasp of the issues, but he could not reach a decision. He could anathematize Chicago and the philistia that seemed inseparable from it; but he could also visualize the futility awaiting the expatriate at the end of his quest. He saw that he must either reconcile himself to Chicago or pay the enormous price exacted of the expatriate for his alienation. Fuller knew that there was still time to reflect, but the moment could come for him, as it had for Gregorianius, when his very indecision would decide for him. Meanwhile, like the Chevalier, Fuller could "still congratulate himself on his exemption from the burdens of wealth, the chafings of domestic relations, the chains of affairs, the martyrdom of a great ambition, and the dwarfing provincialism that comes from one settled home" (184). But what of the future?

VIII   Comparisons

Spurred by the praise that was being given *The Chevalier of Pensieri-Vani,* Fuller quickly wrote a sequel during the summer of 1891. Immediately, *The Chatelaine of La Trinité,* in which Fuller said he "meant to do for the Alps,—French, German, Swiss and Italian—what its predecessor had done for Italy itself,"[10] was accepted by Gilder for publication as a serial in *The Century Magazine* during the summer of 1892 and for release by the Century Company in book form immediately after the last installment of the serial. Gilder wished to make the format of the book in every way comparable to the Century's splendid edition of *The Chevalier of Pensieri-Vani.* He employed George Wharton Edwards, a promising young illustrator who had travelled extensively in Europe, to execute the cover design and the illustrative sketches.[11]

In *The Chatelaine of La Trinité,* Fuller duplicated many of the devices which had proved successful in *The Chevalier of Pensieri-Vani.* In addition to the resemblance between the titles, Fuller's admirers would have recognized his practice of using chapter titles consisting of a place name followed by a phrase more or less descriptive of the incident to be narrated. The vast outpouring of obscure place names, the utter absence of dialogue, and the allegory suggested by such character names as Aurelia West, Fin-de-Siècle, Tempo-Rubato, Baron Zeitgeist, Professor Saitoutetplus, and Mdlle. Pasdenom are strongly reminiscent of the earlier book. More familiar than any other feature, however, would have been Fuller's relaxed, by turns faintly humorous, openly satirical, and richly decorative, even poetical prose. Outwardly, at least, *The Chatelaine of La Trinité* is a recognizable companion piece, in almost every way as elegant and distinguished as its predecessor.

Despite the apparent similarities, an examination of the two books reveals basic differences which may best be understood in terms of Fuller's attitude toward his material. The charm of *The Chevalier of Pensieri-Vani* derives in large measure from Fuller's close, personal affection for such characters as the Chevalier and Prorege. If, on occasion, he gently satirized them, he also deeply sympathized with their tastes, their opinions, and their notions about the good life. When, in *The Chatelaine of La Trinité,* he changed the sex of his leading characters, they cease to be expressions of ideas and behavior which Fuller personally approved; instead, they reflect, to a degree at least, the hostility that Fuller felt toward women. As a consequence, *The Chatelaine of La Trinité* becomes less a work of "idealistic travel-fiction" and more a conventional novel. The Chatelaine and Aurelia West become bolder, more realistic characters than the Chevalier and the Prorege; but Fuller achieved these qualities at the sacrifice of part of the charm that Norton and Lowell had found exceptionally attractive in *The Chevalier of Pensieri-Vani.*

Fuller's decision to change the locale of his sequel from Italy to Switzerland paralleled the shift in characters and widened the distance between the two volumes. The central fact is that Fuller did not react to Switzerland as he had to Italy.[12] In 1880, when Fuller, after six months in Italy, had crossed into Switzerland, he had found the towns clean and the Alpine scenery imposing, even grand; but he could not hide a feeling of disappointment. The peaks of the Alps, however spectacular, did not move Fuller so powerfully as did the beauty and historical associations of the museums, churches, and hillsides of Italy. Except for the mountains, he found nothing in Switzerland that he particularly wanted to see; and eleven years later, as he was writing *The Chatelaine of La Trinité,* he had no deeply felt, nostalgic "after-thoughts" about Switzerland. This failure to make a strong, personal response to the new locale resulted in a more conventional, realistic, and objective approach toward his material than he had taken in his first book. Again, to obtain the new effect, he surrendered part of what had made *The Chevalier of Pensieri-Vani* a minor classic.

The more involved Fuller became with material that was not deeply grounded in his own emotional preferences, the more closely his book approximates the contemporary novel form. Fuller's exquisite delight in the atmosphere of Italy, his affectionate attitude toward his characters, the frequent repetition of primary themes, and the evenness of his prose style contribute a measure of unity to the almost plotless *The Chevalier of Pensieri-Vani;* but the nature of his attitude toward his material prompted him to abandon some of these devices in writing *The Chatelaine of La Trinité* and compelled him to devise a suspensive plot to connect the episodic chapters. The presence of a suspensive plot effectively separates the two books.

Whatever Fuller intended to accomplish in writing a sequel to *The Chevalier of Pensieri-Vani,* he actually produced in *The Chatelaine of La Trinité* an outwardly related but basically different book. In place of the atmosphere, charm, and romance of the earlier book, Fuller offered in his second book firmly drawn characters, objective descriptions of mountain scenery, and a suspensive plot. *The Chatelaine of La Trinité* thus represents a movement away from the "idealism" of Henry James toward the realism of William Dean Howells; but, during the process, Fuller's writing suffers a distinct loss in charm, in freshness, and in vitality.

IX   The Metamorphosis of the Chatelaine

The central action of *The Chatelaine of La Trinité* arises from the determination of Aurelia West, a young lady from Rochester, New York, to fashion Bertha, the Chatelaine of La Trinité (a courtesy title) and a modest, unpretentious Swiss girl from an aristocratic family, into Miss West's own idea of a European noblewoman. Aurelia's successes—and her failures—provide a unifying motif for the series of sightseeing tours which she makes with the Chatelaine and her godfather, the Governor (a courtesy title), to Lucerne, Constance, Salzburg, the Dolomites, Meran, Verona, Bellagio, and, finally, La Trinité.

Aurelia West, whose function in *The Chatelaine of La Trinité* parallels that of George W. Occident in *The Chevalier of Pensieri-Vani,* is the most vigorous character yet created by Fuller. Beside her, Occident appears a mere theorist, the product of the same society that spawned Miss West, yet in no sense a zealot seeking to realize his ideas in either Italy or Arcopia. Aurelia is a far more frightening specter, for she energetically works to "corrupt" the naturalness and simplicity of her European sister: to make Bertha adopt American ideas about the importance of women. Occident, to a degree at least, remains open to persuasion; but Aurelia has long since passed the point of discussion. She is all the more vicious because she is intelligent; she is all the more dangerous because she is single-minded and energetic.

Although Miss West's efforts to "Americanize" Bertha meet sporadic opposition from Fin-de-Siècle and from the Marchese of Tempo-Rubato, Aurelia's most formidable opponent is the Baron Zeitgeist, a keen observer of both American and European institutions. Zeitgeist maintains that no society as urban and industrial as that emerging in America could fail to develop a kind of aristocracy of privilege and that in America this *"aristos"* is taking the form of an "incredibly widespread, close-knit, firm-rooted, all-pervasive, and ultra-tyrannical . . . aristocracy of sex" (110). Speaking for Fuller, and anticipating his criticism in *The Cliff-Dwellers* and *With the Procession,* Zeitgeist delivers a sweeping broadside against the tyranny of the American woman:

> What was American society . . . but a magnificent galley in which husbands and fathers toiled at the oars, while wives and daughters sat above in perfumed idleness? He had met a gentleman in New York, the possessor of twenty millions of florins, who had told him that he was working for his board and clothes—he seemed to be employing a recognized phrase. This unfortunate toiled more incessantly than his meanest clerk, and had absolutely not a single pleasure; but his wife and daughters, along with a hundred others like them, resided in a great hotel without duties, insensible of any obligations, and unoccupied except by their own diversions (110).

Nowhere does Miss West validate the justness of Zeitgeist's characterization better than in the incident at Bellagio. Having made substantial progress in her efforts to convert Bertha to American notions of womanhood, Aurelia needs only to compel the homage of the three young noblemen. In the luxurious villa of Tempo-Rubato's family, a single white flower of marvelous beauty blooms in the center of a small, stone-encircled pond. The blossom, unique and exceedingly precious to the young man's father and mother, becomes, in Aurelia's eyes, the test of her triumph. By taking advantage of the hospitality and manners of her host and the young noblemen, Aurelia forces

Fin-de-Siècle to wade into the pool to pick the flower for the Chatelaine.

Neither the Chatelaine nor Miss West is seriously concerned about the havoc that Fin-de-Siècle is obliged to wreak upon the quiet lily pool or his ruined shoes and muddied trousers. These are merely the legitimate tokens of chivalry and are to be viewed with complacency. Miss West, as Fuller wrote, "had always been taught to expect a great deal of the men, to express her expectations unreservedly, and to insist most rigorously upon their fulfilment" (157-58). Aurelia is the daughter of the American industrial and urban democracy. "It was her fundamental belief," continued Fuller, "that the young woman was the corner-stone of the social edifice—the *raison d'etre* of society —almost its be-all and end-all; the spokes of the social wheel all focused in her; toward her every function worked, from her many a function proceeded; she both guarded the gates and sat on the throne—at least that was the way it was in America."

Fuller did not, however, permit Aurelia a complete victory. In the beginning, she has matters firmly in hand because of the admiration of the three young noblemen for the Chatelaine; but, as Aurelia's ideas of womanhood begin to induce a subtle but recognizable change in the Chatelaine herself, the men draw back. From this point, the more vigorously Miss West attempts to compel their worship of Bertha, the more openly the men rebel. In the concluding chapter, which takes place at La Trinité itself, Aurelia's final moment of triumph turns into defeat because the men refuse to risk their lives on the mountain peak to obtain the sprig of edelweiss necessary to satisfy the whim of the Chatelaine and her high priestess Aurelia West. Each man satisfies his standard of social decorum by sending back to the Chatelaine from a distant city some token which relates both to himself and to the sprig of edelweiss.

Fuller agreed with Aurelia West that sooner or later "Americanization was the impending fate of Europe" (158). The reason is simply that Europe, like the Chatelaine, is willing to be Americanized. He made the point forcefully in the three concluding paragraphs which serve as an epilogue to *The Chatelaine of La Trinité*. A recent visitor to La Trinité has encountered there a group of engineers, a dam across the mountain stream, an iron bridge, and the "muffled shriek of a steam-whistle." As for Bertha, she has left the valley: "The Chatelaine —her way prepared, her path made straight—was now in Paris" (176). Europe has begun to accept the new industrial order, and the simple, natural, unpretentious lady of the modest chateau has now moved to Paris. Europe is in the process of becoming America—becoming Chicago.

X Conclusions

Fuller's first book, *The Chevalier of Pensieri-Vani*, had been conceived out of Fuller's private need to debate the issues which, he felt, were determining the course of his life: Chicago and Italy, Howells and James, the actual and the ideal, the present and the past. Whatever the terms he used and however persuasively he dramatized them, they always resolved themselves back into the relation between Henry Blake Fuller and the society into which he was born, a society which he could neither willingly accept nor totally reject. When he had written himself out, he found he had solved nothing.

By comparison, his second volume, *The Chatelaine of La Trinité,* though still a very personal document, is less emotionally charged, less intense, and less an agonized expression of the conflicts which tormented him. The loss in personal involvement, however, yielded a compensating gain in objectivity, and the movement of the setting from Italy to Switzerland freed Fuller from an emotional relationship with his locale. The result is a movement toward an analysis of the effects of the impact of American social standards upon European notions of the good life.

Although Fuller ostensibly wrote two books about Europe, a considerable portion of *The Chevalier of Pensieri-Vani* is actually a thinly disguised analysis of American society, and in *The Chatelaine of La Trinité* he allowed the American material to overshadow almost everything else. In the earlier volume, America is present in merely a passive role. In his second book, the New World is actively crusading—exporting, along with its material goods, the social values of an industrial and urban society; and, Fuller believed that in doing so it was destroying much of the Europe that he cherished. If there is any doubt about Fuller's position, his second book makes clear that he liked both the older America that had already virtually disappeared in Chicago and the older Europe that he feared was about to vanish because of the influence of the new American order. His admiration for the order that was dissolving as he wrote made him all the more effective a critic of the new society that he saw evolving to take its place.

CHAPTER 5

The Inhabitants of the Clifton

Although Fuller wished to return to Europe immediately after completing *The Chatelaine of La Trinité,* delays in negotiations with Gilder detained him in Chicago throughout the fall of 1891. By January 5, 1892, however, when he sailed from New York, he had made final corrections in the typewritten copy of *The Chatelaine of La Trinité,* concluded arrangements with Gilder for its serialization in *The Century Magazine,* and agreed to write for Gilder several pieces about Spain. Fuller was away six months. He spent six weeks in France, all of March in Italy, and April and May in Spain. On June 29, 1892, he was back in Chicago.

I Architecture at the Chicago Fair

In actual writing, the literary results of Fuller's third trip to Europe are unimpressive. He kept a journal but filled it only with phrases reminding him of his itinerary and indicating topics that might later be expanded. The entries for Spain, perhaps the major literary objective of his entire trip, are the briefest of all, consisting merely of names of places and hotels. In London, he wrote a short article about the architectural features of Westminster Abbey for *The Century Magazine* and in Spain a very slight piece entitled "Holy Week in Seville."[1]

Either while in Spain or shortly after he had returned to Chicago, Fuller wrote the first chapter of a romance which he called "Our Lady of Light." From his manuscript and from the use he finally made of the material in *Gardens of This World* (1929), it seems clear that he intended to follow the pattern he had established in *The Chevalier of Pensieri-Vani* and in *The Chatelaine of La Trinité.* The best explanation of this venture is that Gilder, who was inclined to consider Fuller primarily a travel writer, had suggested a Spanish volume to accompany Fuller's earlier books. But, after writing about thirty pages, Fuller recognized that the Spanish material was becoming less and less congenial; and, in the fall of 1892, he wisely abandoned the project. The reason for his decision lay partly in his changing concept of fiction and partly in the events associated with the World's Columbian Exposition.

When Fuller returned from Europe at the end of June, 1892, he found that during his six months' absence substantial progress had been made on the construction of buildings for the World's Columbian Exposition. Although few of the structures were then completed, the general layout of the area and the broad architectural features of the whole could be discerned—enough to reveal to Fuller the essential wisdom of the original design for the grounds imagined by Daniel H. Burnham and John W. Root. Every effort was being made to advance construction so far as possible before the special dedication services on October 20, 1892, although the official opening of the Fair would not take place until May 1, 1893.

During August and September, 1892, Fuller wrote for the Chicago *Record* a series of articles about the architecture of the Exposition. For the most part, he spoke approvingly, even enthusiastically, of the achievements of the architects. With the decision to adopt the classical style for the buildings adjacent to the formal basin, called the Court of Honor, Fuller was in complete agreement. The harmony of style resulting from the "dominant Roman note," asserted Fuller, referred back with "a straight and unbroken directness to the great structures of Caligula and Nero."[2] The total effect produced by the "spaciousness, homogeneousness and splendor" of these buildings exceeded the earlier expositions in Philadelphia and in Paris and "might almost be compared with that presented by the Palatine hill in the days of the early Roman emperors." Even more important, thought Fuller, was the certainty that what was being done at Jackson Park would leave a permanent mark upon American architecture. The advances made, he declared, "should be sufficient to show that artistic America is moving along at an equal pace with industrial America."

Looking back over the development of American architecture during the preceding decades, Fuller noted that ever since the Philadelphia Centennial, which he had attended as a boy, American architecture had been suffering through years of "straying, stumbling and unsatisfactory experimenting." Now, the architects of the Fair were bringing the art back to "the right path—or, at least, *a* right path."[3] So far as Chicago was concerned, however, Fuller's praise of the architectural achievements in the Court of Honor was a double-edged compliment. The buildings in this area, comprising what he called the southern section of the grounds and including the buildings of agriculture, machinery, electricity, liberal arts, and administration, were, he said, "in the hands of Boston and New York,"[4] that is, in the hands of Richard W. Hunt and a small group of his associates. The northern section, which Fuller found much less worthy of praise, was being designed by Chicago architects whose aim Fuller characterized as "in the direction of the informal, the novel, and the picturesque."

The example of excellence set by Hunt, Fuller implied, might serve as a valuable guide and pattern not only for the Chicago architects for the Fair but also for those who were designing buildings in downtown Chicago. Evaluating the progress of architecture in Chicago since the great fire of 1871, Fuller admitted that it displayed "considerable invention and ingenuity"[5] in the solution of the technological problems underlying the construction of skyscrapers; but he denied that the Chicago architects had created "a distinctive American style." The direction of his thinking is evident from his remarks about style:

> If an architectural style were the product of one man or the result of one day we of Chicago should be close upon its track; for we have at least one designer of notable independence and originality. John W. Root excepted, no man has perhaps put a stronger imprint on our local architecture than Louis H. Sullivan. . . . But an architectural style is not the product of one man, however inventive, nor of one day, however rapid. It is the product of a race, of an epoch—the slow result of evolution and selection. There is one historical style which is safe, stable, serviceable and universally adaptable. This is the style of the Romans, manipulated for modern uses by the Italians, French and Spaniards of

the renaissance. And it is this style—in its various aspects—that
been selected for the great work of the Fair.[6]

Thus, although Fuller's knowledge of architecture compelled
him to admit the resourcefulness, even genius, of Chicago men
in devising the remarkable technical innovations which made
possible the modern skyscraper, he refused to acknowledge
that Chicago had developed an "American style."

The skyscraper simply would not fit into Fuller's historical
perspective. He would not concede that, since the Roman era,
civilization had changed so fundamentally that the classical
style could no longer be serviceable. Fuller would not even
grant that the skyscraper had evolved necessarily out of the
patterns of life created by an urban, industrial, and technological civilization. From his position, William Le Baron
Jenney, John W. Root, and Louis H. Sullivan were gifted and
resourceful innovators; but they could scarcely be regarded as
pioneers in a new architectural style.

Fuller's attitude was consistent with many of his other views.
His architectural sympathies lay with an earlier America that
found its literary center Harvard Yard, Brattle Street, and
Concord and its architectural affinities in the classical style
urged upon the country by Thomas Jefferson in the early days
of the republic. Like Daniel Burnham, Fuller hoped, and may
have expected, that the Roman style would eventually prevail
in American urban architecture;[7] and he was correct in his
estimate that the influence of the World's Columbian Exposition would count in this direction.

Five years later, however, in his celebrated essay "The Upward Movement," Fuller admitted that, although classicism
had made gains outside the city, the movement had failed in
Chicago itself. Fuller concluded that Chicago's streets could
never become beautiful. "The associated architecture of the
city," he wrote, "becomes more hideous and more preposterous
with every year, as we continue to straggle farther and farther
from anything like the slightest artistic understanding."[8] Fuller
could find beauty neither outside nor inside these structures, and
he never fully grasped the strength of the bond between the
skyscraper and the urban civilization that was rapidly becoming the norm of American life.

II   Toward *The Cliff-Dwellers*

Ever since Fuller had written his essay "Howells or James?" his own interests and outward events had been pushing him toward a direct confrontation with Chicago. In this essay, he had acknowledged that Howells' insistence upon American subjects for American writers was sound doctrine, yet Fuller had promptly written an imaginative, romantic volume of "idealistic travel-fiction" which was much closer to James than to Howells. Between the appearance of *The Chevalier of Pensieri-Vani* and *The Chatelaine of La Trinité,* Howells had published *Criticism and Fiction;* and Fuller, at least by implication, had reacted in *The Chatelaine of La Trinité* with what may be understood as a statement of his dissatisfaction with the theory of realism.

After characterizing realism as "close observation, accurate transcription, nothing more," Fuller declared that the observation became "more than close; it was searching—yes, it was even remorseless; it spared nothing, since everything served its purpose equally." For Fuller, "the great thing in art was not to know, nor even to feel, but to divine."

> Observation was good, assuredly; sympathy was better, even indispensable; but what, after all, was to be placed before the exercise of the constructive imagination freely working its own way on to its own end?—an imagination that seized on a word, a gesture, a flower, a flash of color, a simple succession of sounds, and by means of a few humble, external facts called out from within such a multiplicity of correlated fancies as resulted at last in a drama, a fresco, a symphony, a cathedral. The genesis of a work of art was the genesis of the echo; one word is spoken and twenty are evoked in reply—only no reverberations were to be looked for from empty nothingness.[9]

Fuller believed he stood on solid ground: his position was valid for all the arts. The dramatist, the painter, the composer, the architect, and the writer found observation and sympathy desirable, even necessary; but these factors always remained subordinate to the imagination which conceived the controlling idea, the form, of the work of art. In Fuller's opinion, form was the "backbone of art";[10] emphatically, it was the most essential element in architecture and literature.

Despite his arraignment of the shortcomings of realism and his respect for the importance of form, in *The Chatelaine of La Trinité* Fuller was actually approaching, closer than ever before, Howells' position. The prime qualities of *The Chevalier of Pensieri-Vani* had been subjectivity, impressionism, allegory, and idealism. The movement in *The Chatelaine of La Trinité* lay in the direction of objectivity, contemporaneousness, and ordinary life. While much of the earlier volume related to the ancient civilizations of Italy, Fuller in his second work had concentrated upon the European present and hinted of the future. Both books had relevance to Chicago; but, whereas in the former Chicago appeared as a distant, shadowy place, in the latter it loomed as a female ogre prepared to make Europe over in the image of Midwest America.

Although the line of Fuller's literary development ran straight from Europe to Chicago, the decisive factor in his decision to "cross over" was neither James nor Howells but the depth of Fuller's own commitment to Chicago. He had made three extended trips to Europe, in which he had tasted the satisfactions of an expatriate's life; but he had shown no disposition to remain abroad. Separated, as he wished to be, from the mainstream of Chicago life, Fuller had no desire to accept the alienation that would have been his as an expatriate, and perhaps also a dilettante, in any foreign country. Whether he liked it or not, Chicago remained the baseline from which he measured deviation up or down. Chicago was his home; and all the stimulus that Fuller needed to make him confront it directly in fiction was provided by the World's Columbian Exposition.

III Form and Plot of *The Cliff-Dwellers*

In January and February, 1893, while the final preparations were being made for the opening of the World's Columbian Exposition, designed to show the glories of Chicago to the rest of the nation and the countries beyond the seas, Henry Blake Fuller wrote *The Cliff-Dwellers*, the most celebrated novel about Chicago ever to be published. In a brilliant introductory chapter, he described Chicago as a city of towering cliffs rising from great canyons dug deeper each succeeding year by the rush of "an ever-increasing prosperity" (1). The surrounding countryside, which Fuller characterized as "the rugged and erratic plateau of the Bad Lands," is a treeless, shrubless, arid, and air-less country, a "mighty but unprepossessing landscape," that is vaguely visible from the cliffs "through swathing mists of coal-smoke."

Of the cliff-dwellings, Fuller named only three—the Tacoma, the Monadnock, and the fictional Clifton. The Tacoma, designed by William Holabird and Martin Riche, had been completed in 1889; while the sixteen-story Monadnock, the work of Burn-ham and Root, had been finished as recently as 1891. Both of these skyscrapers, conceived and executed in the utilitarian, functional, commercial architecture of the Chicago school, were considered the last word in urban office-buildings; and Fuller was painfully conscious of the vast difference between these "modern monsters" and the beautiful classicism of the Court of Honor being built at the World's Columbian Expo-sition in Jackson Park. Fuller was equally aware that the prose style that he had used to render the romantic charm of Italy would not serve in dealing with the raw, commercial life of Chicago. For the Chicago book, he employed a plain, bare style that seemed to him to be appropriate to solid masses of the cliff-dwellings he was using as his central symbol.

The reference to the Tacoma and the Monadnock build-ings helped to increase the reality of Fuller's fictional skyscraper, the eighteen-story Clifton, whose name accorded with his practice of using names having allegorical significance. In describing the Clifton, Fuller emphasized the three most note-worthy features of the new skyscrapers—the multiplicity of windows, the stairways, and the elevators: "Its hundreds of windows glitter with multitudinous letterings in gold and in silver, and on summer afternoons its awnings flutter score on score in the tepid breezes that sometimes come up from Indiana. Four ladder-like constructions which rise skyward stage by stage promote the agility of the clambering hordes that swarm within it, and ten elevators—devices unknown to the real, aboriginal inhabitants—ameliorate the daily cliff-climbing for the frail of physique and the pressed for time" (4).

The Clifton, Fuller implied to his readers, is the focal point of the story he was about to narrate. Its inhabitants, numbering about four thousand persons, constitute a microcosm of Chicago business life. "It includes," declared Fuller, "bankers, capitalists,

lawyers, 'promoters'; brokers in bonds, stocks, pork, oil, mort-
gages; real-estate people and railroad people and insurance people—life, fire, marine, accident; a host of principals, agents,
middlemen, clerks, cashiers, stenographers, and errand-boys; and
the necessary force of engineers, janitors, scrub-women, and
elevator-hands" (4-5). Since the Clifton is "complete within
itself," concluded Fuller, "it will be unnecessary for us to go
afield, either far or frequently during the present simple succession of brief episodes in the lives of the Cliff-dwellers."

As a symbol from which the plot and the meaning of his
novel could have evolved, the Clifton might have provided
Fuller with both an enveloping form and a controlling idea to
which everything else in the novel might have been related. In
one of his small, pocket notebooks, Fuller once observed that
"as regards fiction, I personally am in favor of the sociological
novel rather than the psychological novel"; and he then continued, significantly, "instead of a searching and indelicate
analysis of the individual, I would favor the study of a group of
individuals in their relation to the community."[11] As a symbol,
the Clifton provided him with an excellent opportunity to
make such a study within the limits of a relatively tight form.
Unfortunately, Fuller was often willing to content himself with
the general outline or structure of a form in both literature
and architecture and to ignore the relation of specific details to
the larger units of his form. In *The Cliff-Dwellers*, the result
of these tendencies is that, although the novel opens and closes
with the Clifton, much of the action and many of the characters have no direct relation to the building or its occupants.
Only in a broad sense was Fuller making a study of a group in
relation to the Clifton-community, and only very generally
does the Clifton or the "cliff-dwellers" impose a controlling
form upon his novel.

Despite the latitude which Fuller permitted himself in developing the form, the Clifton must be considered the organ-
izing symbol of the novel. His statement, made years later,
that the book was supposed to ask the question of whether a
young man would be wiser to marry a girl who, though shallow
herself, comes from an attractive family, or to marry a girl who,
though having a splendid character herself, has disreputable
relatives, may hardly be taken as the underlying idea of the

work.[12] George Ogden, the young man of the novel, is not even aware until the last third of the book that this question might become a problem for him.

Although the point of view is that of a central figure, George Ogden, Fuller sought primarily to invent incidents and situations which would establish the relationship of his characters to the life of the city. As a newcomer to Chicago, Ogden offers a convenient vehicle for Fuller's comments; because, as Ogden endeavors to improve himself financially and socially, he inevitably meets different types of persons whom Fuller could conveniently utilize to document his case against Chicago. Consequently, Fuller devoted as much attention to Ogden's associates as to Ogden himself. This approach, which is similar to Fuller's method in his first two books and which is particularly well suited to the application of realism to fiction, necessarily produces a series of episodes or tableaux rather than a highly unified plot involving one or two suspensive actions which envelop the entire novel.

Of the persons whom Ogden encounters in Chicago, by far the most powerful figure is that of his employer, Erastus M. Brainard, president of the Underground National Bank. An enormously wealthy but thoroughly unscrupulous financier, Brainard has achieved financial success at the sacrifice of his humanity. Without friends, social relations, family life, or a sense of obligation to the community in which he lives, Brainard has become "a financial appliance" (38) instead of a man. In the process he has reduced his wife to a pathetic figure of "abysmal incapacity" (135). Before the final catastrophe, he has disinherited his younger daughter, Mary, who has been victimized by a vulgar and unscrupulous adventurer; and he has utterly destroyed the artistic aspirations of his younger son, Marcus, because he has "not the slightest faculty for business" (98). The older son, Burton, who exhibits his father's vices without his father's shrewdness, risks the entire family fortune upon one daring business "deal," loses, and reduces the family to near poverty. Of the six members of the Brainard family, only the older daughter, Abbie, possesses any qualities of which Fuller could approve; Brainard's all-consuming passion for making money has ruined the others.

In general, Erastus Brainard represents the Chicago of Fuller's father's generation—the Chicago that was driving ahead relentlessly toward the single goal of making money. In the pursuit of this inflexible purpose, Brainard has crushed his wife into abject passivity; but in the succeeding generation—and occasionally even in Brainard's time—there are wives who refuse to be crushed and men who, having amassed a fortune, are willing for the social success of their wives to symbolize their financial success. So long as there is sufficient money, as in the example of Arthur J. Ingles, owner of the Clifton, wives may harmlessly be indulged in what Fuller considered the useless vanities of social competition. In those families where there is not sufficient money, however, the tyranny of sex can become ruinous. Fuller had briefly made this point in *The Chatelaine of La Trinté*;[13] in *The Cliff-Dwellers* he dramatized his criticism much more forcefully in Ogden's marriage to Jessie Bradley.

Although Jessie Bradley's parents have been satisfied with moderate financial success, a modest house in Hinsdale, and limited social pretensions, Jessie aspires to social prominence in Chicago. Almost immediately after their marriage, Ogden learns the cost of competing socially with the enormously wealthy Ingleses. Jessie demands a private carriage, floral displays and professional musicians for her receptions, and expensive furnishings for her parlor. She commissions the fashionable and expensive architect, Mr. Atwater, to design elegant doors for their rented house. Heedless of Ogden's warnings that with his modest salary they cannot match the lavishness of the Ingleses, Jessie continues the extravagances that can lead only to disaster. The death of their baby and her own long fatal illness form a pathetic ending to a marriage already doomed by the competition for social recognition in Chicago.

Ogden's essential mediocrity prevents him from becoming an attractive hero. He represents Fuller's best example of the young man without marked intelligence or moral force who unquestioningly assents to the "system." He comes to Chicago to make his fortune, obtains employment through a letter of introduction, and receives promotions because his employer's daughter feels a romantic attraction for him. His inexperience and lack of perception make possible the impoverishment of his mother and the ruin of his marriage to Jessie. Firmly caught in the web of competition in Chicago, Ogden steals from the bank to pay Jessie's medical expenses; and only the melodramatic stabbing and illness of Brainard save him from criminal prosecution. Ogden's second marriage, at the end of the novel, to Abbie Brainard seems to have more chance of success than his first because of Abbie's firmness of character and not because of any significant change in Ogden. Since Fuller concluded the novel almost immediately after the marriage, the reader has no opportunity to learn what takes place in the future. The issue served Fuller's purpose as one of the many facets of Chicago life that provided grist for his mill.

IV Fuller's Complaint Against Chicago

Each time Fuller returned from one of his long sojourns in Europe, he reacted with greater intensity to the commercial society whose development he had been witnessing in Chicago ever since his childhood. Although Europe had its own deficiencies, still it seemed to have a static society, a sense of the past, and an artistic tradition. Fuller might have acknowledged slight traces of these European institutions in New England, but Chicago had none—and, worst of all, was not ever likely to have them. Herein lay the basis of Fuller's complaint against Chicago. He became convinced that the basic assumptions or premises upon which life rested in Chicago were destructive, or at least inimical, to the qualities which he considered requisite for satisfactory living. At the core of *The Cliff-Dwellers* lie Fuller's disappointment and resentment at what he saw in Chicago. In these terms, the novel is a dramatization of the unhappy effects of acceptance of the values and conditions of life which, Fuller believed, Chicago urged upon the individual.

Large segments of Chicago's population, it must be admitted, escaped Fuller's notice in *The Cliff-Dwellers*. For the most part, his concern was not with the immigrant groups or the workers in the railroads, the stockyards, or the steelmills; and he touched very lightly upon the politician, the educator, or the professional man. Instead, his interest focused upon those of his own class whom he had encountered through his grandfather and father, his experiences at Ovington's and in the bank, and his handling of the family's rental properties. For them, the Clifton was an admirable symbol, and their particular circumstances and role in the life of the city Fuller was well qualified to dramatize in his novel.

Fuller was impressed by the extremely fluid nature of this portion of Chicago's citizenry. In his earlier books, he had written approvingly of a society in which the individual's status was established from birth or by the service he rendered in a world where "quiet and contentment and domesticity"[14] were the cherished values. In Chicago, Fuller was irritated by the fact that nothing was established. Everyone was a newcomer, and everyone had come for the single purpose of getting rich as rapidly as possible. Ogden reflects Fuller's attitude when he asks: "Is there anybody in this town who hasn't come from somewhere else, or who has been here more than a year or two?" (12). No one has any long-standing relationships; no one is respected for any other reason than because of his money.

The fluidity of Chicago society encouraged an exaggerated emphasis upon what Fuller considered unimportant trivialities. The right name, the correct address, the proper associations became matters of undue concern to a class of people whose money scarcely covered the thin veneer of their lowly origins. The sketch of Shayne is a good illustration of Fuller's point:

> Now Shayne, for example, began life with a fruit-stand—Jim Shayne they called him. The fruit-stand developed into a retail grocery, and Jim Shayne (about the time of the Fire) became J. H. Shayne. The retail grocery expanded into a wholesale grocery, and the sign read, "James H. Shayne & Co.," and the firm made money. But the day dawned when his wife began to figure at dances and receptions—her own and those of other people—as Mrs. James Horton Shayne, and when his daughter's wedding was not far away, with all the splendor that St. Asaph's could command. This was no juncture for laying undue stress on the wholesale grocery business; it seemed worth while to become identified a little less closely with mercantile circles and a little more closely with financial circles. Shayne & Co. went right on —both routine and profits; but the High-flyers' National was started, and James Horton Shayne was more likely to be found on La Salle Street than on River Street (33).

From somewhat similar motives, Ogden's prospective brother-in-law, Eugene H. McDowell, selects an office in the Clifton next to that of Arthur J. Ingles, the financially influential owner of the building. The desire to live in a new, expensive, and fashionable neighborhood prompts a number of characters—Ogden and his wife, Mr. and Mrs. D. Walworth Floyd, and Mr. and Mrs. Burton T. Brainard—to change their places of residence.

Of the characters in *The Cliff-Dwellers* who struggle to climb the ladder of success in Chicago, none embraces the axioms of materialism more eagerly than Cornelia McNabb. Even Fuller conceded her energy, resourcefulness, and shrewd opportunism. Having come to Chicago from Pewaukee, Wisconsin, not long after Ogden has arrived from New England, Cornelia begins as a waitress in Ogden's West Side boarding house. Through the "intelligence office," she obtains a job in the restaurant of the Clifton. "I'm going to get along, let me tell you," exclaims Cornelia to Ogden; "I haven't jumped on to this hobby-horse of a town just to stay still" (63). In her off-duty time, Cornelia takes courses in shorthand and typewriting; and she scans the newspapers for the names of those society leaders whom she is ambitious to emulate. She has only admiration for Mrs. Arthur J. Ingles, Chicago's acknowledged society leader, and for Mrs. Granger S. Bates, who, like Cornelia, had once taught school. As society "dudes" at the top, Cornelia approves of them.

Within a few weeks, Cornelia has left the Clifton restaurant to become an independent, or free-lance, stenographer who works for such important persons as Burton Brainard, now vice-president of the Underground National, and D. Walworth Floyd of the Massachusetts Brass Company. She continues to read the papers and to dream of the day when her name and picture will appear in the society columns. When she begins to attend the theater with Burton Brainard, Cornelia's goal seems very close. Cornelia's marriage to Burton Brainard—she insists that it take place in a church—brings the newspaper publicity for which she has longed; and, after their return from the honeymoon, she gloats over the cards announcing she would be "at home" on the "Thursdays in September." As Mrs. Burton Brainard, she can meet society on her own terms. "I expect I shall cut a pretty wide swath" (226), Cornelia acknowledges to herself.

For three months Cornelia enjoys her French Renaissance

chateau on Lake Shore Drive and the stream of socially important people who exchange invitations with her. At the end of that time, Burton's financial failure deals her happiness a severe blow. Cornelia vows to rise again. "I'll capture Cecilia Ingles yet!" (314). At the end of the novel, Cornelia, at the opera, watching the Atwaters and the Ingleses take seats in their box, murmurs to herself: "Just you wait. Burt's smart and I'm careful, and we shall catch up to you yet!" (323).

For Fuller, the career of Cornelia McNabb provided an excellent example of both the good and the bad in Chicago. Her abundant energy, her determination to succeed, and her practical shrewdness characterized much that was wholesome in Chicago. What troubled Fuller was the fact that her one objective in life was to occupy a place in society by the side of Mrs. Arthur J. Ingles. Fuller would not have objected to this ambition if Mrs. Ingles had represented anything other than a naked, unashamed materialism based solely upon a money-success. For this kind of goal to be accepted as the desideratum of life for women seemed to Fuller the negation of all that was worthwhile in civilization; indeed, it hardly seemed civilization at all.

Bad as Cornelia's lack of worthwhile goals seems to be, Ogden's standards are scarcely any better. Cornelia herself knows that Ogden's position is essentially the same as her own. When she learns he has moved to a better address, she remarks, "I see now why you moved. I don't blame you. I'm trying to get along, too. We're both in the same boat" (71). If Ogden has any other goals in life beyond money-making, Fuller failed to indicate them. Despite Ogden's assertion that Cecilia Ingles is "only a beautiful myth" (119), he admits in the final paragraph of the novel that she has only too much reality. "He knew that she was Cecilia Ingles," wrote Fuller; "and his heart was constricted by the sight of her. It is for such a woman that one man builds a Clifton and that a hundred others are martyred in it."

Chicago's failure, according to Fuller, arose principally from the absence of adequate goals for the ambitions and energies of its intelligent, middle-class citizens. The single goal that it did provide, material success symbolized by the ownership of real estate, social snobbery, and social climbing, crushed the individual more often than it uplifted him because it enslaved all his faculties in a competition for a worthless prize. The race to make money prevented the individual from being recognized for what he contributed to society and instead approved only what the individual took from society. Repeatedly, Fuller dramatized the devastating effect of the commercial spirit upon the citizen's family life, upon his cultural life, upon his community life, and even upon his religious life.

Though not a bitter book, *The Cliff-Dwellers* struck a hard blow of protest against a city then putting forth its best efforts to demonstrate to a nation that it had progressed both culturally and artistically as well as materially; but in its moment of pride, Henry B. Fuller, one of the few Chicago writers with a national reputation, could find virtually nothing about the city to praise. Even the costly enterprise of the World's Columbian Exposition received a chilling blast, as Fuller advised the young men in Chicago to shun architecture as a career and instead "go in for mining or dredging, or build bridges, or put up railway sheds, if you must; but don't go on believing that architecture nowadays has any great place for the artist. There won't be another Fair until long after you are dead and gone" (97).

Although he had written hastily and had not said all that he wanted to say, Fuller had dealt honestly with the issues as he saw them. He had taken the technique of realism a step farther than Howells had gone, but Fuller stopped short of the areas of life which Robert Herrick and Theodore Dreiser were to enter. The kind of searching analysis of Chicago's "robber barons" which Herrick and, more particularly, Dreiser were to make in the years ahead held no interest for Fuller. His was largely a personal reaction to a city which he felt was moving in the wrong direction.

CHAPTER 6

The Procession in Chicago

Howells expressed his admiration for *The Cliff-Dwellers* in a perceptive review which appeared in *Harper's Bazaar*,[1] and in a private letter he urged Fuller to keep on writing about Chicago, "whether you like it or not."[2] Howells saw that, although Fuller had already done for Chicago what no one— Howells modestly excluded his own *The Rise of Silas Lapham*— had yet done for New York or Boston, Fuller had the potential to write an even better novel about Chicago. Good as *The Cliff-Dwellers* was, it had certain very real blemishes.

I A New Approach

Most of the faults of *The Cliff-Dwellers* arise from the fact that Fuller wrote it in anger and in haste. Spurred by years of resentment against the competitive, pecuniary standards of Chicago and by the contrast between the classical features of the White City being constructed in Jackson Park and the Black City he knew downtown, Fuller failed to take the time to solve the artistic problems of his material. Unhappily, he allowed the brilliant architectural symbol of the Clifton, which should have given form to the entire work, to assume in the final third of the novel a subordinate place to the melodramatic events in the Brainard family and the marital experiences of young Ogden. This artistic flaw was compounded by Fuller's willingness to crowd his novel with a horde of minor characters and secondary issues and by his eagerness to attack every possible facet of the commercial life of the city. Toward almost every character in the novel, Fuller's antagonism was uncompromising. In every respect, *The Cliff-Dwellers* was a harsh book.

No one would deny that Fuller had produced a forceful arraignment of the ills of Chicago, but the fact remains that the novel would have carried more conviction had not the central focus of the work been blurred by the multiplicity of themes and had his principal message not been obscured in a general polemic. Fuller could do better, and he knew it. He wrote Howells that *The Cliff-Dwellers* was "not definitive"; rather, he said, it represented merely "the wrist-and-elbow exercise of a new man who hopes to 'get his hand in' for better things."[3]

By the winter of 1893, when he began to write *With the Procession,* Fuller had gained a measure of perspective on the Chicago scene. Without changing his basic attitude, he decided to approach his material from a slightly different point of view. In *The Cliff-Dwellers* he had harshly condemned the city and almost everyone associated with it, but he now determined to focus his attention upon those whose allegiance was to the old Chicago but who were forced to live in the new era. This new approach permitted him to draw upon the experiences of his own family in Chicago and, most importantly, to feature characters with whose plight Fuller, himself, sympathized. For this reason, the characters in *With the Procession* exhibit a warmth and general attractiveness that had been conspicuously absent in his first novel of the city.

Fuller's solution to the problem of form was equally as fortunate as his change in point of view. The relentless pressure upon Chicago citizens to "keep up with the Joneses" had been but one of many matters which Fuller had discussed in *The Cliff-Dwellers.* In writing *With the Procession,* Fuller selected the theme as the controlling or form-giving idea for the novel, rephrased it to broaden its application, and rigidly subordinated everything in the novel to the development of its implications. The high degree of organic unity exhibited by *With the Procession* results very largely from his concentration upon this single thematic device.

II The Marshall Family

With the Procession may best be characterized, in Fuller's own words, already quoted, as a "study of a group of individuals in their relation to the community." In this instance, the group consists principally of the Marshall family, who, in 1893, the time setting of the novel, abruptly perceive that they have for years been standing still while their contemporaries in Chicago have moved far ahead of them. As might be expected, the family's predicament is felt much more forcibly by the younger generation than by the parents. Although the characters are types, their sharply contrasting attitudes and ideas help to make them appear highly individualized.

The elder Marshalls, David and his wife Eliza, who resemble Fuller's own parents, belong to the "old settlers" of Chicago, whose city never really changes despite the fire and the phenomenal growth of the population. In 1893, theirs is still the Chicago of 1860, an Arcadia that over the years has merely grown larger, noisier, and richer—different only in degree and not in kind.

The Marshalls, who have failed to keep up with the procession, live in "a sedate, stable, decorous old homestead" (20), which Eliza and David built just before the Civil War; but they have made no effort to modernize the furnishings, redecorate the rooms, or replace the worn carpets. In the back yard, even the currant bushes which have always provided the fruit for the annual jelly-making are succumbing to the smoke and cinders which have already subdued the flowers and cherry trees of the formerly attractive garden. The neighborhood, once fashionable, has now been almost engulfed by commercial establishments and slums. The Marshall house is the one remaining bastion of respectability.

Years ago, Eliza Marshall abandoned her place in Chicago society. Once active in social affairs, she has now become "a house-keeper cumbered and encompassed by minute cares largely of her own making" (5-6), and her social activities in recent years have been confined solely to attendance at the annual game dinner. In 1893, she is hurt because the Marshalls do not receive an invitation to the affair. Like the Marshall horse-drawn carryall, Eliza makes "no pretense to fashion" (3); and she has been left behind by society.

David Marshall, a far more sympathetically drawn character than Erastus Brainard in *The Cliff-Dwellers*—perhaps, in part, because of David's resemblance to Fuller's own father—has made a fortune of three million dollars in the wholesale grocery business. Beside Brainard, who remains to the end a ruthless, tyrannical, though forceful robber baron, Marshall appears as a tired and kindly man. He reminded Fuller of a dray horse: "You imagined him to have been caught early, broken to harness at once, and kept between the shafts ever since. It was easy to figure him as backing into position with a sweet and reasonable docility. . . . Now, at sixty, he seemed still to be traveling over the same long straight road, blinders at his eyes, a high wall on either side, no particular goal in the dusty distance, and an air of patient, self-approving resignation all about him"(19).

Like Silas in Howells' *The Rise of Silas Lapham*, David has committed only one questionable deed in his career; but he has been unable or unwilling to accommodate himself to the more progressive or aggressive business methods of his contemporaries. He realizes that he is falling behind in both business and society, and he dies in the bitter knowledge that most of his children have little respect and no love for him. David, as well as his wife Eliza, is a member of the "old guard"; inclined to be selfish and self-centered, they exhibit no feeling of obligation to the community, though both are unhappy when they realize that the community has passed them by.

Eliza and David would have been content to live in the old way, had not their eldest daughter, Jane, forced the issue. Jane is not very atractive. Tall and lean, her back "narrow and of a slab-like flatness," Jane's eyes "have the peculiar stare which results from over-full eyeballs when completely bordered by white," and "her long fingers show knotted joints and nails that seem hopelessly plebian" (5). At thirty-three—she was born in the same year as Fuller himself—Jane admits to her mirror, "I guess I'll give up trying to be beautiful, and just be quaint" (18). She seems destined to become, as she later describes herself, "a benevolent old maid with a capacity for society when occasion offers" (201). Her intellectual honesty, however, more than compensates for her appearance. Unquestionably, Jane is the most forceful and the least selfish of all the Marshalls.

Prompted by her desire to advance the social fortunes of her younger sister, Rosamund, Jane insists upon a formal debut for her; and, when their mother opposes the party, Jane's sarcastic retort reveals her awareness of the family's shortcomings. "No," declares Jane, "don't let's have any party or dance or reception or anything at all. Not even a two-by-four tea. Don't let's try to be anybody or know anybody, or give anything or be considered anything. Let's go right on rusting and vegetating . . ." (34). Asked for an explanation of her vehemence, Jane exclaims: "I mean that I'm simply tired of being a nothing and a nobody in a family of nothings and nobodies. . . . I'm tired of sitting on the fence and seeing the procession go by. Why can't *we* go by?" Jane's efforts to persuade her family to keep up with the procession become the mainspring of the plot.

The other members of the Marshall family play subordinate roles in the novel. Both Alice and Roger have already married and broken away from the family home. Neither is a very attractive person. Alice, now Mrs. Robinson, "a contentious blonde," whom Fuller characterized as "the radical, the innovator of the family" (35), lives in Riverdale Park, where she informs her mother and sisters, "more happens with us in a week than happens with you in a year" (37). Roger, a self-righteous lawyer, devotes all of his energies to amassing a fortune from his legal practice and from speculations in real estate. Fuller remarked that Roger's was "a hot and vehement nature, but it burned with a flame blue rather than red" (267). Hard and calculating himself, Roger has no patience with those who enjoy leisure or display interest in esthetic matters. Neither Roger nor Alice is interested in attaining a place in Chicago society, and only occasionally do they influence the actions of the other members of the Marshall family.

Rosamund and Truesdale, the two youngest Marshalls, actively support Jane's plans to regain the family's social prominence. Rosamund, or Rosy, particularly, determines to catch up with the procession. Although selfish, egotistical, inconsiderate, and often petty, Rosy has enough beauty and vivaciousness to make her acceptable in society. Perhaps more than any other person in the family, Rosy succeeds in climbing the social ladder, though Fuller intimated that her marriage to the snobbish Englishman, Arthur Scodd-Paston, falls short of the triumph for which Rosy had hoped.

Richard Truesdale Marshall is a much more complex character than Rosy. At the end of his sophomore year, he abandons his studies at Yale University to seek culture and adventure on the Continent. His itinerary allows him to spend considerable periods supposedly studying philosophy at Heidelberg University, painting in Paris, voice in Milan, and archaeology in the Peloponesus. On his return to Chicago, which takes place in the opening pages of the novel, Truesdale politely refuses any connection with his father's grocery business; on the contrary, his ambition is to become "the pioneer of the leisure class" (86) in Chicago. Socially attractive because of his sophistication, his amateur talent for singing, and the facile cleverness of his painting, Truesdale slides easily into the life of a dilettante.

Much to his disappointment, Truesdale finds the cultural resources of Chicago woefully inadequate to his demands. The shop window takes the place of the European picture gallery, the theaters scarcely offer one satisfactory play each month, and the concerts are totally unreliable. Worst of all, Chicago has absolutely nothing to offer in place of the European "promenade" and the European café. Truesdale summarizes its deficiencies in the remark: "No journals, no demi-tasse, no clientèle, no leisure . . . nor any excursions; nor any general market; nor any military; nor even any morgue. And five francs for a cab. *Quelle ville!*" (141). In boredom verging on despair, Truesdale finally exclaims: "I declare, . . . take it all together, and it's enough to drive a man to—business. . . . For what can a man of leisure do, after all, in such a town as this?" (294).

Jane Marshall had hoped that Truesdale would help her to pull the family out of its social and civic lethargy. "Between him and me," she tells herself while awaiting his return from Europe, "something *may* be done. Pa'll never do anything to get us out of this rut; nor ma. Neither will Roger nor Alice" (17). Truesdale does little to support Jane's efforts though he realizes the truth of her assertions. The motivating force of the family—and of the plot of the novel—is Jane Marshall. "It was her office," wrote Fuller, "to keep the family from disintegration" (26).

III Ways to Overtake the Procession

In her campaign to help her family catch up with the procession, Jane Marshall finds her strongest ally in Mrs. Granger Bates, the former Sue Lathrop, who, through the years, has retained a sentimental attachment for David Marshall, one of

her favorite beaux in her girlhood. An "old settler" herself,
Mrs. Bates has kept up with the procession and exerts great
power in the social circles of Chicago. With her support, and,
at times, direction, Jane undertakes to launch Rosy in society,
to stimulate David Marshall to assume an active role in civic
and business affairs, and to persuade him to build a new home
for the Marshalls in a fashionable section of Chicago. The ad-
vancement of these projects constitutes the plot of *With the
Procession*.

Of all these aims, Rosy's debut is the easiest to accomplish.
Having assured herself that Rosy is clever "and just the least
little bit selfish and inconsiderate" (65), essential qualifications
for social popularity, Mrs. Bates arranges a modest tea as the
best means of introducing her to society. "This whole function,"
the realistically minded Mrs. Bates informs Jane, "has only one
object. That object is to show your sister for five minutes to
Cecilia Ingles" (128). As Mrs. Bates knows, social success means
acceptance by Mrs. Ingles, the acknowledged leader of Chicago
society. Rosy passes the test brilliantly.

Relying upon his own experience and the speeches which
Jane writes for him, David Marshall begins to take a more
active role in public affairs; but he stubbornly resists all efforts
to induce him to give or build something for the city that will
make him recognized as a public benefactor. Mrs Bates's sug-
gestions include a dormitory at the university—she and Mr.
Bates are giving Susan Lathrop Bates Hall for women—a school
or a hospital, or even a substantial contribution to the symphony orchestra or perhaps an endowment for a theater. Mrs.
Bates's urgings are seconded by David's close friend, Tom Bingham, an architect and builder, who urges him to "do something for yourself and for the town" (159). Jane hopes that her
father will provide the money to build a home for working
girls. During his lifetime, David refuses to support any of these
projects. In his will, however, he has made a bequest for a college
building; but, shortly before his death, he transfers the entire
amount to Jane, who, he believes, is the only one of his children
who really loves him. Jane decides that the money shall be
used to erect the building anyway.

When a group of business men offer to purchase the Marshall
house in order to build a warehouse on the property and when

a gang of neighborhood thugs attack the family coachman, David and Eliza yield to the pressure from Jane and Rosy to build a new house in a better neighborhood. Esteeming "convertibility before domesticity" (205), Roger selects a site three miles to the south, on Michigan Avenue, near the old city limits; and David engages Bingham to find an architect and build the house. Although Jane questions this reversal of the usual procedure, she helps the architect with the plans and later inspects the construction with Bingham. Months later, in the final chapter of the novel, David, now dying, and his family move on a cold day in November to the chilly, inhospitable, still unfinished and mostly unfurnished house.

A plot more consonant with Howells' tenets of realism may scarcely be imagined. If anything, Fuller had outdone Howells; for Fuller, in *With the Procession*, had cut his path closer to the commonplace events in the lives of ordinary people than Howells had been able to do in either *The Rise of Silas Lapham* or *A Hazard of New Fortunes*. Fuller's great feat lay in avoiding the melodramatic while at the same time imposing upon his novel a high degree of form through the use of a plausible central idea or theme which rigidly controlled and subordinated both characters and events. Thus Fuller solved the major artistic problem which confronted the realists: the necessity of steering a course between a contrived plot and the formlessness of literal transcription. For his achievement, Fuller won the lasting admiration of Howells. "At present," wrote Howells, reviewing *With the Procession* in June, 1895, "we have no one to compare with him in the East, in scale and quality of work."[4]

IV Mrs. Granger Bates

In Mrs. Granger Bates, whom Howells described as "the chief triumph of the book,"[5] and David Marshall, Fuller exemplified, respectively, those who not only keep up with the procession but actively seek to lead it and those who lag behind because they are either unwilling or unable to assent to new goals and new standards of conduct. The constant factor, or frame of reference, against which both Mrs. Bates and David Marshall must be measured, remains Chicago; and the issue between these two characters lies at the very center of Fuller's novel.

Mrs. Bates seems to have many good qualities. Howells considered her "a mass of good sense, and good will, and good principle."[6] The daughter of a boss carpenter, Mrs. Bates, like many of Chicago's leading citizens, has moved from rags to riches within a single generation. Through her own efforts, ambition, and vitality, she has "arrived," and she is determined to maintain her place. She and her husband, who began his career as an inventor, Mrs. Bates observes to Jane Marshall, "have fought the fight . . . and we have come out ahead" (70). She continues:

> And we shall stay there, too; keep up with the procession is my motto, and head it if you can. I *do* head it, and I feel that I'm where I belong. When I can't foot it with the rest, let me drop by the wayside and the crows have me. . . . When I led the grand march at the Charity Ball I was accused of taking a vainglorious part in a vainglorious show. Well, who would look better to play a role than I, or who has earned a better right to play it? There, child! ain't that success? ain't that glory? ain't that poetry?

The fact is that Mrs. Bates's good qualities, as this speech ironically suggests, are directed toward the wrong goals. Consistent though they may be with the objectives and standards of the procession in Chicago, Mrs. Bates's notions of success, glory, and poetry fall far short of Fuller's own concepts.

In one sense, at least, Mrs. Bates is not to blame. Chicago has failed to provide the proper ends or outlets for her energy and her ambition. Chicago has elevated external forms over the inner growth of the individual. Her collection of paintings, for example, under certain circumstances might have been a worthwhile activity for a person of wealth; but for Mrs. Bates, it becomes only a means of keeping up with the procession. Her motive for collecting may be grasped from her explanation of Mr. Bates's purchase of a Corot. "I let him go ahead," she declares, "for, after all, people of our position would naturally be expected to have a Corot" (68).

An important point in Mrs. Bates's creed is that she always wants to learn. "I *want* to learn," cries Mrs. Bates; but the reader soon realizes that Mrs. Bates wants to learn about paintings because it is fashionable to know about them. Similarly, she wants to learn to play the music of Grieg, Lassen, and Chopin, not for the pleasure their compositions give her, but because the ability to play them is required for membership in the Amateur Musical Club.

Mrs. Bates's home offers an excellent illustration of the compromises which her ambition to keep up with the Chicago procession forces her to make with herself. Escorting Jane Marshall through the rich, ornate rooms of her mansion, Mrs. Bates openly admits that her house exists for show rather than for living. In the tremendous music room, with its concert-grand and handsomely bound scores of the classics, Mrs. Bates casually observes that she has not sat there in a month. In the library, where the works of the standard authors are kept in cases that she cannot unlock, Mrs. Bates remarks, indicating a beautiful writing desk, "really I don't suppose I've written two lines at that table since it was put there" (69). Upstairs, in the lavishly decorated bedroom, Jane learns that the bed "isn't to *sleep* in; it's for women to lay their hats and cloaks on" (71). Finally, after passing through the office, where Mrs. Bates dictates to her secretary, the truth about her hostess unfolds to Jane:

> She found herself in a small, cramped, low-ceiled room which was filled with worn and antiquated furniture. There was a ponderous old mahogany bureau, with the veneering cracked and peeled, and a bed to correspond. There was a shabby little writing desk, whose let-down lid was lined with faded and blotted green baize. On the floor there was an old Brussels carpet, antique as to pattern, and wholly threadbare as to surface. The walls were covered with an old-time paper whose plaintive primitive-ness ran in slender pink stripes alternating with narrow green vines. In one corner stood a small upright piano whose top was littered with loose sheets of old music, and on one wall hung a set of thin black-walnut shelves strung together with cords and loaded with a variety of well-worn volumes. In the grate was a coal fire. Mrs. Bates sat down on the foot of the bed and motioned Jane to a small rocker that had been re-seated with a bit of old rugging (72).

Here is Mrs. Bates's retreat, the place where, secure from the other marchers in the procession and safe even from her own servants, Mrs. Bates can be herself. Here she can have the furniture from her old home, play the old songs she enjoys, prop the window open with a hairbrush, and admit that she prefers a bed of portulacca to orchids, American beauties, and formal beds of gladiolus.

Mrs. Bates's notions of civic responsibility are consistent with her social creed. She believes that persons who have great financial wealth should give to the community. In the new order of Chicago, "the man who enjoys the best position and the most consideration," she informs David Marshall, "is not the man who is making money, but the man who is giving it away . . ." (114). But she exposes her actual motives, as she continues: "As I have said so many times to Mr. Bates, 'Make it something that people can *see*.'" Mrs. Bates and her husband are giving the Susan Lathrop Bates Hall for women to the university, not because they wish to support education, but because they will be known for their contribution. In a similar fashion, Mr. Bates is contributing to the symphony orchestra, not because he enjoys music, but because, declares Mrs. Bates, "a man of his position is naturally expected to support a great artistic enterprise" (115).

In view of the duplicity of motive practiced by Mrs. Bates, William Dean Howells' admiration of her "good principle" seems more than generous. The fact is that Mrs. Bates's efforts to keep up with the procession in Chicago have been made at the cost of her integrity. That she may have been well meaning does not keep her from being, in several respects, a fraud and a hypocrite. As Mrs. Granger Bates of Chicago, the leader of the procession, with all her millions, her mansion, and her charities, she can scarcely be what she claims to David Marshall: "I *am* the same old Sue" (112).

V David Marshall

Tom Bingham, the architect, energetically supports Mrs. Bates's efforts to persuade David Marshall to contribute a building to Chicago. Like Mrs. Bates, Bingham tries to appeal to Marshall's own self-interest as well as to his sense of civic responsibility. "Do something for yourself," exclaims Bingham to Marshall, "and for the town" (159). As examples of worthwhile projects, Bingham mentions telescopes, model lodginghouses, statues, and fountains. In his reply, Marshall ignores the benefit that might accrue to himself in the form of publicity. He is not convinced that the public deserves a gift. In the past twenty years, he has watched the public of Chicago become "a banding together of petty officials with their whole contemptible following: steerage-rats that have left their noisome holds to swarm into our houses . . ." (161). The presence of this group of foreigners in his own neighborhood and his inability to secure redress of his grievances against them in the city courts have combined to make Marshall build a new home in a different area.

Neither Bingham nor Mrs. Bates has offered any specific civic reason why Marshall should make a contribution to the city. In answer to Marshall's antagonism toward the public, Bingham can only reply that "the noblest mountain in the world . . . is only rocks strewn over with sticks and stones. But if you will just step back far enough to get the proper point of view—well, you know what the painters can do with such things as these" (297). Marshall's answer reflects not only his bitterness but perhaps that of Fuller as well: "I can't step back, Bingham. I started here; I've stayed here; I belong here. I'm living right *on* your mountain, and its sticks and stones are all about me. Don't ask me to see them for anything else; don't ask me to call them anything else." In Marshall's opinion, the man who meets the requirements of his family and "the legal exactions of the community" has done enough.

Marshall remains, to the end of his life, one of the "old settlers." He exhibits the virtues and the limitations of those who came to Chicago to make their fortunes in the 1850's and 1860's. With this group, to which his own father and grandfather belonged, Fuller could sympathize. He admired their unwillingness to compromise either with the incoming foreign element or with those who sacrificed their principles to keep up with the procession. Their most serious limitations, Fuller believed, were ultimately to be attributed to the fact that Chicago placed too great a value upon business success and encouraged its wealthy citizens to undertake civic projects only for selfish reasons. Most of all, Fuller lamented the fact that men like David Marshall could become mere machines for making money and live lives alienated from any right relationship with their families, the community, and the world of beauty.

VI The Face of Chicago

Fuller's criticism of Chicago, though apparent in his portrayal of such characters as Mrs. Bates and David Marshall, is perhaps most bluntly expressed through the character of the dilettante, Truesdale Marshall. His comments, in fact, repeat Fuller's own characteristic ideas about the city; and to this degree, Truesdale may be said to act as Fuller's spokesman in *With the Procession*. Shortly after Truesdale returns from Europe, he visits the site of the World's Columbian Exposition which had closed during the previous week. "It is good," observes Truesdale, "better than I could have thought—better than anybody over there could be made to believe" (86). Fuller, too, had returned from abroad to find the Exposition much better than from the vantage point of Europe he had believed possible; and Fuller, like Truesdale, hoped that the spirit of the White City would be transferred to the nearby Black City, "over which it was to hover as an enlightenment—through which it might permeate as an informing force" (87).

In the passage which immediately follows in the novel, Fuller mingled his own estimate of Chicago so closely with that of Truesdale that there can be no doubt of the complete agreement between the sentiments of the author and the comments of the fictional character:

> "Good!" he thought; "there's no place where it's [the spirit of the White City] needed more or where it might do more good." The great town, in fact, sprawled and coiled about him like a hideous monster—a piteous, floundering monster, too. . . . Nowhere a more tireless activity, nowhere a more profuse expenditure, nowhere a more determined striving after the ornate, nowhere a more undaunted endeavor towards the monumental expression of success, yet nowhere a result so pitifully grotesque, grewsome [*sic*], appalling. "So little taste," sighed Truesdale; "so little training, so little education, so total an absence of any collective sense of the fit and the proper! Who could believe, here, that there *are* cities elsewhere which fashioned themselves rightly almost by intuition—which took shape and reached harmony by an unreasoned instinct, as you might say?"

Truesdale's reference to cities "elsewhere" could only mean the cities of Europe whose plan and pattern of development **Fuller** had admired during his trips abroad.

The lack of harmonious shape for the city was only a symptom of a much deeper deficiency at the center of Chicago life. Everywhere Fuller saw energy and activity, that is, motion, but the motion both in private and in public life seemed to Fuller to be directed toward the wrong goals. In both *The Cliff-Dwellers* and *With the Procession,* Fuller's criticism of Chicago always returns to the question of the fullness of the individual's life in the society of his contemporaries. In re-viewing *The Cliff-Dwellers,* Howells recognized that the face of Chicago in Fuller's fiction was also the face of New York or Boston or Philadelphia. "Perhaps nine-tenths of the whole city life of America," wrote Howells, "can find itself glassed in this unflattering mirror."[7] Everywhere Americans were striving after the false god of Mammon or worshipping the bitch-goddess Success. Fuller and Howells were among the last writers even to hope that the trend might be reversed. The younger men, represented by Theodore Dreiser, would respect Fuller as a pioneer in realism but would look at Chicago from a totally different point of view. On them, Fuller's influence, nevertheless, would be strong, so strong, in fact, that in 1932, in an article on realism, Dreiser rejected Howells as "too socially indifferent" while hailing Fuller as "the father of American realism."[8]

VII Critical Reception

Shortly after the appearance of *With the Procession* in May, 1895, Fuller saw that the new work had won approval. Eastern critics joined their Midwestern colleagues in praising the work for its artistic and realistic portrayal of Chicago. In the *Atlantic Monthly,* the reviewer expressed the widespread opinion that "Fuller has shown a deft touch in the handling of his material; he has fancy, and he has, above all an artistic sense which forbids him to bear on too hard."[9] Writing for *The Critic,* Lucy Monroe described the book as "realism, but realism lit by an imagination which grasps the deeper motives of action, the inner issues of thought,"[10] an opinion echoed by Lilian Bell in *The Chap-Book.*[11] Generally, *With the Procession* was con-

sidered less forceful than *The Cliff-Dwellers* but notably, as
James Huneker declared, "finer in its art, its characterization
and development."[12]

Inevitably, the reviewers made comparisons between Fuller
and Howells, or Garland. Huneker, for example, wrote: "It sees
Chicago in just the happiest perspective. The conflict of the old
and new social order could not have been better done by Mr.
Howells. . . . In Fuller we have at last met the American novelist. . . . He has culture, courage, convictions, sees his country
from the objective viewpoint—something that travel alone can
confer—is not parochial like Mr. Howells, nor semi-savage like
'Ham' Garland, and is first and last dramatic."[13]

Howells, himself, generous in his estimate of Fuller's achievement, noted that Fuller's "perfect intelligence" was the most
remarkable aspect of the book. "He isn't fumbling in the dark,
at any moment," wrote Howells; "he isn't guessing at clues; he
isn't building up figures from bits of personality, gathered here
and there as any alien observer might gather them. He was
himself born to the manner of the people he depicts, and the
wonder in this case is that he is able to regard them sufficiently
aloof to get them and their belongings into such true perspective."[14]

The only jarring note came from Charles Eliot Norton, whose
earlier promotion of *The Chevalier of Pensieri-Vani* had greatly
advanced Fuller's career and whose opinion Fuller valued
highly. Although Norton had been reluctant to advise Fuller,
Norton had written, in October, 1893, that the realism of *The
Cliff-Dwellers* was implicit in *The Chevalier of Pensieri-Vani*.
"It is the man of imagination, the poet," declared Norton, "who
alone sees things as they really are; it is the writer who has
a natural genius for style who can present with equal worth
the charm of Italy, or the repulsiveness of that aspect of Chicago
which you depict."[15] In making this observation, Norton tacitly
acknowledged the validity of Fuller's concept of the "style
absolute" that had allowed him to write in one style for a
romantic work like *The Chevalier of Pensieri-Vani* and to adopt
a decidedly different style for *The Cliff-Dwellers*. With apparent
approval of Fuller's line of development, Norton compared
Fuller favorably to Howells.

In 1895, however, after reading *With the Procession,* Norton voiced the reservations that he may have held privately since the publication of Fuller's first Chicago novel. Norton's remarks, in fact, raised once more questions which Fuller had debated but never completely solved. After expressing appreciation for the book, Norton wrote:

> It is a painful book, hardly less so than "The Cliff-Dwellers," but this is at once evidence of its worth and of its power. It raises a somewhat serious question, whether such life is fit subject for literary art, and whether the record of it is the best work which you can do for Chicago—for it is after all for Chicago that we are all working,—Chicago, or New York, or Denver City, however our democracy may call its palace-hovels. To be brief, I hold with the poets and the idealists; not the idealizers, but those who have ideals, and, knowing that they are never to be realized, still strive to reach them and to persuade others to take up the same quest. I believe that your "Chevalier" has done more for Chicago than any of the true Chicagoans whom you have given to us, "twice as natural" as life. . . .[16]

Unknowingly, Norton had rephrased the old "Howells or James?" issue which Fuller had debated at the outset of his career. What Norton suggested disturbed Fuller not because he thought Norton wrong but because he was inclined to agree. "What is a poor duck to do?" asked Fuller.[17] The doubt became one of the factors which kept Fuller from following the vein he had opened in *With the Procession*. Twenty-three years would elapse before he would write another novel dealing with Chicago.

CHAPTER 7

Progress of the Arts

To many observers, the World's Columbian Exposition of 1893 offered proof that the beginnings of culture had already come to the booming Midwest metropolis. Henry Blake Fuller, the historian of the "upward movement" in Chicago, characterized the Fair as "a kind of post-graduate course for the men at the head of Chicago's commercial and mercantile interest; it was the city's intellectual and social annexation to the world at large."[1] Few observers would have denied that the Fair had greatly strengthened the civic consciousness of Chicago, broadened the outlook of its leading citizens, and made patronage of the arts, at least temporarily, fashionable.

I The Upward Movement

On Chicago's small group of creative artists, eager for encouragement and recognition, the Exposition exerted what Harriet Monroe called "an incalculably inspiring force."[2] They shared the belief of Charles Eliot Norton who wrote that "the Fair, in spite of its amazing incongruities and its immense 'border' of vulgarities, was on the whole a great promise, even a great pledge."[3] Among many of its literary men, including William Morton Payne, George Ade, Hobart Chatfield-Taylor, Peter Finley Dunne, Charles Fisher Browne, and Melville E. Stone, the Fair generated an atmosphere of intense optimism. Influenced directly by their enthusiasm, Hamlin Garland decided to move his home from Boston to Chicago. Even Fuller's harsh and grimly pessimistic outlook was momentarily softened by the general hopefulness of the time.

In the larger context, of course, the Exposition, dramatic and impressive as it was, must be considered as merely one of the evidences of a general "upward movement" among the arts that had begun in Chicago during the 1880's and persisted well into the 1890's. The course of this movement Fuller traced in

his article "The Upward Movement in Chicago." Calling attention to the educational character of the new interest in the arts,
Fuller placed major emphasis upon the cultural institutions
which had either been activated or vastly expanded during these
years. Among them he named the Civic Federation (largely
political in its activities but in a broad sense a cultural influence
as well), the University of Chicago, Hull House, the Public
Library, the Newberry Library, the Crerar Library, the Chicago Orchestra under the direction of Theodore Thomas,
the Chicago Conservatory, the Art Institute, the various artistic
clubs, *The Dial,* and the Central Art Association. The thrust
of the "upward movement," as well as the rapidity with which
cultural developments came to Chicago, may be grasped from
the fact that in the single year 1892—the year in which Fuller
wrote *The Cliff-Dwellers*—the Art Institute was built and the
Public Library, the Newberry Library, and the University
of Chicago were either established or placed in operation.

Against this background of a Chicago seeking to educate
itself culturally, trying as Fuller said, to catch up to "the bare
decencies"⁴ and to acquire cultural institutions which more
fortunate cities like Boston and Philadelphia had already
possessed for generations—against this background of hopefulness, cultural ferment, and artistic excitement—Fuller's own
activities in the later years of the 1890's must be measured. From
1892 to 1894, when he was writing *The Cliff-Dwellers* and
With the Procession, Fuller was the most important writer in
Chicago. By 1900, he was beginning to fall behind; and by
1918, when he wrote his next novel about Chicago, Fuller
could hardly be said to be in the literary procession. The loss
of his vitality remains the central enigma of Fuller's biography
during his later years.

II   Fuller's Associates

Despite shyness and an almost obsessive desire for personal
privacy, Fuller enjoyed friendships with most of the talented
architects, painters, sculptors, writers, editors, and publishers
who worked in Chicago during the 1890's and the opening years
of the twentieth century. Although they knew very little about
his private life, they welcomed him to their studios or offices

because of his interest in their careers and his perceptive comments about their work. With perhaps the exception of Lorado Taft, Fuller was better informed on artistic subjects than anyone else in the art colony; and for many years Fuller and Taft were the acknowledged leaders of the celebrated association of artists called the Little Room.

The Little Room became Fuller's substitute for the European café whose absence in Chicago Truesdale Marshall had lamented in *With the Procession*. This loosely organized, informal gathering of artists, according to Anna Morgan, began in 1893 at the suggestion of Lucy Monroe.[5] Its name was taken from a story by Madeline Yale Wynne about a room that appeared and disappeared at intervals, but the Little Room was intended to provide a weekly meeting place for those interested in art. At first, the club met on Friday afternoons, from four to six o'clock, in the studio of Bessie Potter, the successful sculptress of graceful miniature "statuettes" and a close friend of Henry Blake Fuller. In 1899, however, after Charles C. Curtiss had converted the Studebaker warehouse (on Michigan Avenue at the corner of Van Buren and very close to the heart of Chicago's Loop district) into the Fine Arts Building, the Little Room was moved to the studio of Ralph Clarkson, the painter, on the tenth or top floor. There, when the group assembled for tea every Friday afternoon after the concerts of the Chicago Symphony Orchestra, Fuller was rarely absent.

Throughout the years, the membership of the Little Room fluctuated in accordance with the fortunes of the art colony. Besides Garland and Taft, those closest to Fuller included Anna Morgan, the dramatic coach and theater director; Frederick Richardson, Ralph Clarkson, and Charles Francis Browne, painters; Allen and Irving Pond, architects; Bessie Potter, sculptress; Hobart Chatfield-Taylor, Lucy and Harriet Monroe, Herbert S. Stone, Mrs. Elia Peattie, James Taft Hatfield, and Ralph Fletcher Seymour, writers and publishers. Although Fuller visited them at work, their presence at the meetings of the Little Room explains why Fuller valued this group above all other clubs or societies in Chicago.

After the turn of the century, the quality of its membership gradually declined. Fuller, Garland, Taft, Browne, and Clarkson remained; but, as early as 1907, Garland, realizing that New York had drained off many of the most gifted members of the Little Room, proposed to establish a new, larger, more formally organized group open to laymen as well as artists. Garland named the new group the Cliff-Dwellers after Fuller's novel. Fuller steadfastly refused to join it, probably because of his distaste for the formality, bigness, and institutional atmosphere that he felt would be inevitable in such a club.[6]

During the heyday of the Little Room in the 1890's and the first decade of the twentieth century, Fuller, Taft, and Garland, easily the most distinguished members of the group, were bound together by strong personal friendships as well as artistic interests. (In 1899, Garland married Zulime Taft, Lorado Taft's sister.) For more than twenty years, the three men, unless prevented by illness or absence, exchanged ideas or criticisms with one another several times each week. In 1916, Garland's decision to leave Chicago lessened the frequency of their contacts but in no way diminished the strength of their friendships.

In Lorado Taft, Fuller found a congenial companion whose artistic theories paralleled his own. Taft (1860-1936), the son of a professor at the University of Illinois, had gone to Paris to study sculpture about the same time Fuller had made his first European pilgrimage. In 1886, after six years abroad, Taft returned to teach modeling at the Chicago Art Institute. A versatile and competent rather than great sculptor, Taft first attracted widespread attention for his companion pieces, "The Sleep of the Flowers" and "The Awakening of the Flowers," placed at the entrance to the Horticulture Building of the World's Columbian Exposition. Later, he became celebrated for such massive, pictorial fountains as "The Spirit of the Great Lakes," outside the Art Institute of Chicago; "The Fountain of Time," on the Midway in Chicago; and the "Columbus Fountain" in Washington, D.C. Critics praised the tremendous statue of the American Indian "Blackhawk" at Oregon, Illinois, and the beardless "Lincoln" at Urbana, Illinois. During his lifetime, his most popular composition was the group of figures entitled "The Blind," a representation of a scene in Maeterlinck's drama of the same name.

Both Fuller and Taft staunchly advocated the classical style in art. By their simplicity, openness, and chastity, Taft's sculptures consistently reflected a strong influence of Greek forms. To Garland's plea for a distinctly American sculpture, Taft pointed to the ugliness of the popular American soldiers' and sailors' monuments in which the sculptors had attempted to reproduce in literal fashion the service uniforms of the subjects. Sculpture, Taft insisted and Fuller agreed, should be pictorial but also symbolic. As Fuller perceived, Taft increasingly strove to leave "the merely decorative side of sculpture behind him" and to suggest with restraint in line and nobility of feeling the universal truths of human experience.[7] Upon these principles Fuller and Taft were completely united, and so long as Taft continued to select American subjects for his sculpture, Garland approved the result if not the theory behind it.

Considered handsome, affable, and scholarly by his contemporaries, Taft delivered hundreds of lectures on sculpture and painting to stimulate popular appreciation of art through the Midwest. A frequent visitor at Taft's Midway Studios in Chicago and at Eagle's Nest Camp on Rock River, where Taft was the guiding spirit of the summer art colony, Fuller maintained a steady, helpful interest in all of his friend's activities. In 1903, while writing his *History of American Sculpture,* Taft took full advantage of Fuller's skill in expression, his immense knowledge of art history, and his sound critical judgments. With meticulous care, Fuller read the manuscript and corrected the proof sheets both of this volume and Taft's later *Modern Tendencies in Sculpture* (1917), as well as many short essays and articles which Taft wrote to promote the cause of art.

Fuller's willingness to promote the careers of his friends, perhaps to the detriment of his own, helps to explain the remarkable friendship that ultimately developed between Garland and Fuller. At first the two men were cool toward each other. As the champion of western local color, Garland could hardly have been expected to admire either *The Chevalier of Pensieri-Vani* or *The Chatelaine of La Trinité;* nor, in 1891, would Fuller have reacted favorably to *Main-Travelled Roads.* But Garland was impressed by *The Cliff-Dwellers,* and Fuller was flattered by Garland's warm words of praise early in January, 1894. That Garland was arriving from Boston, the home of William Dean Howells, also counted with Fuller. The following month, at Garland's suggestion, the two men met for the first time.

Fuller, then working hard to finish *With the Procession,* was hardly a man to attract Garland. Recalling their first meeting, Garland noted that Fuller "wore at this time a full brown beard and carried himself with fastidious grace, a small, alert gentleman who resented the mental and physical bad smells and the raucous noises of his native town."[8] Garland was at a loss to understand him. "He studied me at our first meeting," continued Garland, "with bright eyes aslant as if only half liking my appearance, whilst I felt in him something puzzling and remote." For a time thereafter, Garland continued to think of Fuller as a "literary trifler," while Fuller considered that Garland lacked polish and literary sophistication.

In the spring of 1894, immediately after finishing *With the Procession,* Fuller made his fourth trip to Europe, spending a large portion of his time in Italy. He did not return to Chicago until late in October. By that date, Garland had settled permanently in Chicago, joined the Little Room group, and begun to frequent the studios of Lorado Taft. Fuller began to see Garland in a new and different light, and Garland began to appreciate Fuller's immense fund of information on literary and artistic subjects. Despite outward differences in background and education, they possessed the basic attitudes that characterized the literary representatives of Howells' generation. As Fuller's enchantment with Europe began to diminish slightly and as Garland became less a spokesman for radical political and economic theories, the two men solidified a relationship that was to last the remainder of their lifetimes. By the publication in 1895 of Fuller's *With the Procession* and Garland's *Rose of Dutcher's Coolly,* whatever reservations each had held with respect to the other had vanished.

III   The Good Years

The eleven-year period between 1890 and 1901 probably included the best years of Fuller's life. In spite of the occasional claims upon his time from his mother's real-estate dealings, he pursued a busy literary career. He published more than half of his total output of books; he wrote a large number of reviews; and he constantly gave literary advice and often direct assistance to such friends as Clara E. Laughlin, Mrs. Elia W. Peattie, Mrs. Mary Jameson Judah, Hobart Chatfield-Taylor, Lorado

Taft, and Hamlin Garland. His fame as the leading writer of the "upward movement" of the arts in Chicago caused him to be sought out by young writers and artists, editors, publishers, and visiting literary figures. The activity and, at times, excitement were good for him. The demands made upon Fuller helped him, partly at least, to overcome somewhat his habitual shyness. In the meetings of the Little Room, in the studios of Taft, Clarkson, and their colleagues, and in Garland's house, Fuller found that he could always talk freely about Chicago and about art. More than he realized, his own intense activity, the presence of Garland, and the stimulus of Taft helped to expand Fuller's horizons. Fuller was almost beginning to enjoy himself in Chicago.

During these years Fuller's attitude toward Chicago temporarily brightened. If he never reached the sunny, enthusiastic optimism of Taft and Garland, he at least came to view the city in a somewhat more favorable light than he had seen it either in *The Cliff-Dwellers* or in *With the Procession;* and, if he abandoned hope for the acceptance of the classical style in the urban architecture of Chicago, he could certainly recognize the progress the city had achieved in other areas. However critical of the motives of the builders and donors he might become, he could not ignore the recognition of the arts made explicit and tangible in the World's Columbian Exposition, the formation of the Civic Federation, the opening of the University of Chicago, the extension classes of Hull House, the establishment of large libraries, the success of the Chicago Symphony Orchestra, the exceptional quality of the Stone and Kimball press, and the consistently high literary level of both *The Dial* and *The Chap-Book.* Here the record of the decade had been astonishing.

Near the turn of the century, as Fuller reviewed the progress of the arts in Chicago and evaluated the evidence, he concluded that the problem was basically educational. "All the best and most strenuous endeavors of Chicago," he asserted, "whether practical or aesthetic, whether directed toward individual improvement or toward an increase in the associated well-being, may be broadly bracketed as educational."[9] The recognition of progress and the knowledge that the problem was educational, however, did not enable Fuller to make his peace with Chicago. All that he had said earlier in his Chicago novels still remained valid. For Fuller personally the educational strivings of the city meant only that it became slightly less a cultural wasteland.

Fuller never ceased to judge the outward appearance of Chicago and other American cities by what he knew of their European counterparts, a point of view which Garland could never understand. Far more thoroughly than either Garland or Taft, Fuller knew the city itself and reacted vigorously to its external features. To Fuller, the progress of the arts in Chicago meant, as much as anything else, the addition of beauty to the city. Here Fuller found little to praise. In 1901, writing in *The Outlook,* he described Chicago as the newcomer approached it:

> In general, we live beneath a sky within a sky, and our funereal pall, while it occasionally lightens, seldom lifts altogether. Whether the newcomer approaches along the bluffs and ravines of the north, or through the swamps and marshes of the south, or over the wide-stretching prairies of the west, the dun trappings of the Great Horror show from afar. As he rattles along through perky suburban settlements, or honest truck-farms, or half-dried swales and disheveled swamps, the horror grows. Across the wide fields—gay with this year's flowers or somber with last year's weeds—separating the raw huddles of workers' cottages, tangles of telegraph-poles and of trolley-wires lead on the eye toward ugly, shapeless hulks looming above the dingy horizon—foundries, elevators, machine-shops, breweries, factories, ice-houses—detached notes that prelude the great discord to come. Then avenues of tracks, shut in by the shameless backs of things and spanned by grimy viaducts; arrays of mean streets doggedly curtained against the sun and resolutely fighting off the sweet country airs. The heart sinks, the stomach revolts, as, through dirt, dust, grime, soot, smoke, and cinders, the trembling neophyte bumps and jars along toward the besmirched shrine of the two-faced goddess of Bustle and Slouch.[10]

Fuller hoped that the development of city parks would return to Chicago a measure of the natural beauty which man had destroyed and would to some extent compensate for the ugliness of the skyscrapers.

IV Experiment in the Drama

After completing *With the Procession,* Fuller was in no hurry to write another novel dealing with Chicago. He had made his point, and he had no desire to traverse the same ground again. Chicago offered a wide variety of material, but large areas of it Fuller knew himself ill-equipped either by experience or temperament to undertake. He still had no wish to write about the Chicago of the foundries, the stockyards, the slums, the underworld, or politics. Furthermore, he shared, to some degree, Norton's doubts about the value of these subjects for literature; and he was reluctant to be permanently classified as a realist. Even as he wrote the concluding chapters of *With the Procession,* he told Garland that he had "no fixed literary creed" and that he felt "a disposition not to use the same model too many times running."[11] Fuller liked to experiment, and his next book was to be in every respect an experiment.

On October 10, 1895, while declining Albert Bigelow Paine's offer to syndicate his literary production, Fuller declared, "I have written nothing for a year past and have no plans for the future."[12] By the end of the same month, however, Fuller had already finished a brief one-act dramatic fantasy, "O, That Way Madness Lies," for publication in *The Chap-Book;* [13] and by the end of December, he had completed twelve additional pieces for publication in May, 1896, by the Century Company, under the title *The Puppet-Booth.* In April, 1896, he wrote a fourteenth sketch, "The Red Carpet," perhaps intended to be part of this volume but never published during Fuller's lifetime.[14]

Fuller's dramatic pieces resulted primarily from his enthusiasm for the "puppet theatre" of Maurice Maeterlinck and the music of Richard Wagner. The former he may have seen or read while in Europe, and the latter had more than once exercised a powerful emotional effect upon him at Bayreuth. Fuller may also have been stimulated by what Garland called the "Maeterlinck craze" in Chicago and by Richard Hovey's translation of the early Maeterlinck plays published late in 1894 by Stone and Kimball in their "Green Tree" series. This volume included Maeterlinck's "The Seven Princesses," which Fuller characterized as "a real little symphonic address straight from the orchestra."[15] In Fuller's *The Puppet Booth,* the Maeterlinck influence becomes most apparent in the dialogue, symbolism, settings, and thematic exposition, while the influence of Wagner may be seen in both the theme and the employment of musical effects to render emotional nuances.

Reviewers, while approving Fuller's work, related many of the pieces to contemporary literary or musical affairs. "The Cure of Souls," for example, was seen as a protest against Wagner's treatment of the sin-sick soul in *Tannhäuser.*[16] "Northern Lights" was interpreted either as a parody of Ibsen or as "a projection of the author's mind into that of the Norwegian dramatist."[17] "The Stranger within the Gates" was considered a satire upon Anthony Hope's hero Rudolph in *The Prisoner of Zenda,* and "Afterglow" was associated with "the untimely closing of Felix Morris' career in America as a star."[18]

Two of the pieces in *The Puppet-Booth,* "At Saint Judas's" and "In Such a Night," are remarkable for their intrinsic merits and their relation to his earlier and later work. Praised by James Huneker as "magnificently subtle,"[19] and by Israel Zangwill as the only one of the pieces to reach the level of Maeterlinck's plays,[20] "At Saint Judas's deals covertly with the theme of homosexuality which Fuller later developed much more explicitly in *Bertram Cope's Year.* In the play, while a bridegroom and his best man wait in the sacristy of the church of Saint Judas for the arrival of the bride, the best man, who opposes the marriage of his friend, reviews the events of their friendship. At intervals in the dialogue and against the background of the organ and the voices of the choirboys, the eight windows of the sacristy come to life and silently enact successive scenes symbolical of the actions and emotional states of the two men. Near the climax, as the seventh window comes to life, the best man declares, "If she were to come, I should not let her have you. . . . Nobody shall have you" (96); and while "the Deadliest of the Seven Sins hides her face," he concludes, "Our friendship has been too long, too close, too intimate. . . . No one shall come between us." To reach his bride, the bridegroom must kill his dearest friend.

"In Such a Night," the concluding play of *The Puppet-Booth,* brings together, in a setting meant to suggest the Court of Honor at the World's Columbian Exposition, the principal characters of *The Chevalier of Pensieri-Vani* and *The Chate-laine of La Trinité*. As Aurelia West shows the Chatelaine and the Prorege of Arcopia the achievements of her city, she creates marvelously beautiful effects from the light of stars, moons, and meteors upon the basin and the fountains rising from it. Over-whelmed by the sight, the Prorege concedes that Arcopia has been eclipsed; and the Chatelaine declares that for perfection only one other presence is required. When they have departed to admire other scenes, Occident and the Chevalier of Pensieri-Vani alight from a gondola. Like the Chatelaine, the Chevalier, impressed by what he has seen, asks only "to find her here . . . in such a night" (209). After his wish has been fulfilled, the Prorege implies that their union would be "the Greatest Glory of All"; and the play ends as the characters enter a gondola to glide toward the fountains in the basin.

In this piece, Fuller brought together in a setting symbolizing the Chicago Fair the characters through whom he had initially contrasted America and Europe. Earlier the Fair had seemed to Fuller an illustration of what could be achieved by adapting the best of the classical style to American forms and subjects, and in *With the Procession,* he had emphasized the contrast between the classical White City of the Fair and the Black City of downtown Chicago. As he wrote "In Such a Night," the issue continued to be in his mind. In the play, the Chevalier, standing amazed at the sight before him, projects his thoughts to "the city which has reared this majestic manifestation" (208). Eagerly he asks, "How can we figure it save as a place of beauty —compacted of such glorious streets and palaces as must be fit for a right noble people?" After the fashion of Maeterlinck, Fuller made Occident's silence constitute a more powerful answer than he could have made with words.

The title of Fuller's book, itself a glance at Maeterlinck's theory and at the Italian *marionetti* with which Fuller was familiar, indicates that Fuller never intended his plays to be produced by living actors on an actual stage. For most of the pieces, the scenery, musical accompaniment, and lighting effects, combined with the relatively slight action, would have pre-cluded staging. Yet, as Israel Zangwill recognized,[21] Fuller's pieces are in no sense mere literary hackwork. They are experi-ments in the blending of sound, sight, and words to achieve a poetic mood. In them, Fuller returned to the kind of work he had done in his first two books. Unfortunately, excellent as they were, they could only appeal to a very severely limited audience. A year after the publication of *The Puppet-Booth*, Fuller noted that his royalty statements were based upon the sale of less than a thousand copies.[22]

V   Europe Once More

In November, 1896, tired of managing his family's real-estate affairs in Chicago and eager for both new and familiar scenes in Italy, Fuller began his fifth journey abroad, the last he would make until 1924. After meeting Garland in New York to discuss Garland's projected biography of Ulysses S. Grant, Fuller sailed for Algiers, his intention being, as he said, to explore northern Africa as "a mere bit of introductory travel to Italy."[23] By the middle of January, 1897, Fuller had spent five weeks in Africa, which, he declared to his friend Irving Pond, was "worth a good solid six months—so much novelty and variety."[24] Writing to Garland (January 15, 1897) Fuller summarized his itinerary and impressions, "After a rainy fort-night at Algiers, I struck out for the desert of Sahara—I wanted to get warm. I steered for the oasis of Biskra, where they have palms, camels, cock-sure sunrises and sunsets—and the *danse de ventre.*" Timgad, he characterized as the "Algerian Pompeii" and Constantine as, topographically and morally, "the most extraordinary town in the world." He concluded his African tour with a four-day visit to Tunis and Carthage. The people, the scenery, and the ruins were new to him. His letters both to Pond and Garland were enthusiastic.

From Africa, Fuller crossed to Sicily where he spent the last two weeks of January, all of February, and most of March. From Palermo, he traveled to Girgenti, Syracuse, Taomina, and Messina. By the middle of April, he had journeyed north-ward through Rome and Naples as far as Florence where he encountered several of his Chicago friends, including Mrs. Mary Jameson Judah, who was writing her book, and Bessie Potter, whose sculptures were "coming on finely" in the studio of Larkin G. Mead, Howells' brother-in-law. Fuller's correspon-dence shows that he was following closely the literary fortunes of Garland, Howells, and James, both in America and in England, and that he was carrying on an extensive correspondence with various "Little Roomers" in Chicago. His advice to Garland to "take a month in England next fall, to *Save Your Eyes and Ventilate Your Brain*" (May 25, 1897), reflects the cheerful, humorous tone of Fuller's letters.

From Taomina, Sicily, Fuller had announced to Garland: "I have not written one goldarned thing since I came over. Why waste the shining hours in such fashion when there is so much to see and do? Rather let me save my writing for my return to Chicago—a vent for the nervous exasperation that is certain sure to overtake me there" (March 2, 1897). Even with Garland, Fuller maintained a reserve, which virtually amounted to secrecy, about his plans for writing. Characteristically, he refrained from telling Garland outright that he had made the visit to Africa and the extended sojourn in Sicily for the purpose of securing fresh material. In this instance, however, Fuller's silence was motivated not only by his natural reserve but also by his awareness that Garland would not approve the choice of foreign material.

Actually, before Fuller left Italy during the first week in June, to return to Chicago, he had accomplished a considerable amount of work. In addition to his indefatigable sight-seeing, he had read in Sicily a number of Italian novels, particularly those of Antonio Fogazzaro, the Sicilian Luigi Capuana, and Matilde Serao; and from Florence he had dispatched a long open letter to *The Critic* about these and other Italian authors. Very likely he translated the twelve Italian short stories which remained unpublished at his death and Carlo Goldoni's play, *The Coffee House,* which was not issued until 1925. Finally, either while abroad or immediately after his return to Chicago, Fuller wrote a long short story, "The Greatest of These," which appeared in the *Atlantic Monthly* in December, 1897, and subsequently as one of the stories in *From the Other Side.*

The most important literary result of Fuller's travels in 1896-97 lay in his commitment once more to Europe for literary material. Despite his two successful Chicago novels and despite the strong influence of Howells and the urgings of Garland, Fuller now turned away from literary explorations of Chicago. Although he never stated his reasons, certainly Fuller's emotional involvement with Europe and the waning of the "upward movement" in Chicago were powerful, even determining, factors. The decision was to have great significance for his subsequent career, because, by 1918, when he finally published another novel about Chicago, the ideas and attitudes of Fuller and his generation had been largely replaced by those of Theodore Dreiser, Edgar Lee Masters, and Sherwood Anderson. Ironically, Fuller, himself, had failed to keep up with the procession, and he had nothing new and vital to say in the post-World War I era.

Upon his return to Chicago, Fuller resumed his family responsibilities and continued to provide literary assistance to his friends. During the fall and winter of 1897, he acted as literary agent and proofreader for Mrs. Judah who had remained in Europe while her book was being published; helped Garland with the Grant biography; and translated Goldoni's play, *The Fan,* for Anna Morgan.[25] "Guess I was meant for a sort of literary *uncle,*" he wrote Garland; "I find myself more pleased to shampoo the heads of other writers' buntlings . . . than to get down to business and make kids of my own" (June 22, 1897). This remark, though meant facetiously, applies increasingly to Fuller's activities during the next two decades. Before the end of January, 1898, however, Fuller had finished reading the proof of his first volume of short stories which Houghton, Mifflin and Company published early in March.

Fuller's volume, *From the Other Side: Stories of Transatlantic Travel,* includes four stories: "The Greatest of These," "What Youth Can Do," "The Pilgrim Sons," and "Pasquale's Picture." Of the group, only "The Pilgrim Sons" had not been previously published in a magazine. Except for the foreign settings, three in Italy and one in England, a mildly humorous tone becoming in several stories outright satirical, and Fuller's fondness for constructing a story around an idea, the collection may scarcely be said to exhibit any pronounced unity. If, however, the very early (1885) story, "Pasquale's Picture," is excluded, Fuller's narration of the stories from the point of view of a single individual who serves both as narrator and participant in the plot establishes a basic similarity in technique throughout the volume. This device and Fuller's method of employing it in these three stories, which were all written between 1895 and 1897, reflect his continued interest in the work of Henry James.

Aside from their artistic merits, the stories in *From the Other Side* furnish examples of the kind of material Fuller thought appropriate for his writing. In "What Youth Can Do," he chronicled the career of Piero, the gondolier, whose youth and handsome appearance enable him to gain the affections and wealth of the senile Duchess of Dogliano, to purchase the title of Prince of Crassegno, to marry an American heiress who wished to be called Princess, and to win an election to parliament. In the already mentioned "Pasquale's Picture," an Italian woman falls into despair when the photographic likeness of her dead son fades beyond recognition. In "The Pilgrim Sons," Fuller satirized American social climbers and snobs, nonentities in their own right, who return to England to claim kinship with British aristocrats only to find they live in a "sawdust palace."

Because of its subject, "The Greatest of These" is perhaps the most significant story in *From the Other Side*. The autobiographical relationship is established by Fuller's use of the same towns and cities of Sicily and Italy in which he had spent the previous winter. The narrator, an American painter, asserts that "character is the first of things,—except . . . the penetrative portrayal of it" (93); and he boastfully declares that writers employ their art to praise his profound understanding of character. Critical acclaim of his painting, he observes, "never falls below 'penetration,' and often enough it rises to 'divination' " (2). The remainder of his narration not only ironically demonstrates his insensitivity and obtuseness but also portrays, by contrast, Russian and Norwegian characters as modest, perceptive, and altogether admirable persons.

Although the stories in *From the Other Side* embody Fuller's criticism of both the British and the American character, his heaviest strictures fall upon the character traits of his own countrymen. In these stories, Fuller continued to voice his disapproval of many traits he thought characteristic of Americans: social pretense, money values, self-centeredness, and moral and artistic obtuseness.

VI At the Turn of the Century

During the closing year of the century, Fuller's literary activities included work upon a group of political satires, an
appraisal of art in America, and a novel. The three pieces, more
significant biographically than esthetically, relate both to Fuller's
Sicilian experiences in 1897 and to the events of the Spanish-
American War. Indirectly, they recall Fuller's early response
to the conflicting artistic claims of Howells and James. More
directly, they reflect Fuller's lifelong efforts to evaluate civilization in Europe and America.

From the first, the cultivated, fastidious, reserved Fuller had
distrusted democracy. Both in *The Chevalier of Pensieri-Vani*[26]
and in *The Chatelaine of La Trinité,* the characters representing
America failed dismally to establish the advantages of democracy over the paternalism advocated by the Prorege of
Arcopia, the Governor, and Zeitgeist; and in *The Cliff-Dwellers*
and *With the Procession* Fuller applied his criticism of democracy specifically to Chicago. In all four novels, he argued
that democracy had provided neither the greatest welfare for
its citizens nor any real support or encouragement to art. Undoubtedly, Fuller's disappointment in the results of the Chicago
Fair and his trip to Sicily accentuated his feelings, but what
finally prompted him to explode into vicious satire was the
imperialistic policy of President McKinley with respect to the
Philippines.

The New Flag: Satires, a pamphlet of sixty pages, opens with
a quotation from Abraham Lincoln asserting that no man may
rightfully govern another without his consent. The temper of
Fuller's satire, however, may be more accurately discerned from
the opening address:

> "Who will haul down the flag!" McKinley says, and in the pose
> of a righteous defender of our glorious banner, glorious still in
> spite of him, he waits for Congress to make reply. More properly
> he should have said, Who has hauled down the flag, the American
> flag, and put up the Pirates' in its stead?
> "And if we were to answer the question rightly, we should say,
> You have, William McKinley. You hauled down our flag when
> you hauled down our principles."[27]

The flag has become a pirate's flag, continued Fuller, because "you have embraced a pirate's principles. . . . And the sooner you haul it down the better for you."

In the poems that followed, Fuller, in rough, scurrilous invective, attacked President McKinley and the members of his administration, particularly Mark Hanna, Senator Henry Cabot Lodge, Senator Stephen B. Elkins, and Senator Thomas C. Platt. Fuller's sense of outrage was particularly inflamed by reports of the conduct of American soldiers and generals. Of General E. S. Otis, in command at Manila, Fuller wrote:

> 'Tis Butcher Otis and his men,
> Fresh from the Philippine slaughter pen.
> Our Weyler who out-Weylers Weyler
> And viler, if there is a viler.
> Whose coward warfare naught respects
> Nor prisoners nor the female sex.

The reference to Valierono Weyler, whose "Reconcentrado" program in Cuba had been viewed in America as particularly inhuman and atrocious, would have been understood by Fuller's readers as extremely caustic.

The New Flag: Satires, which Fuller had privately printed in 1899, may scarcely be said to have advanced his literary reputation. Fortunately for him, the work passed almost unnoticed in the newspapers and magazines. The blunt invective, which descends nearly to the level of nose-thumbing, appears totally inconsistent with the character and temperament of Fuller. In conversation and in correspondence with his closest friends, Fuller seems never to have referred to these satires; and even Hamlin Garland's private diary contains no mention of them. The inference is that Fuller, having satisfied his conscience by speaking out against democratic imperialism, willingly dismissed what he knew was an inferior piece of work.

Fuller's misgivings about the imperialism of American democracy reinforced his pessimistic outlook upon the future of American art. In "Art in America," which appeared in *The Bookman* (November 10, 1899), Fuller could find little to encourage and much to defeat the American artist. In an analysis strongly influenced by the literary theories of Taine, Fuller noted that the Anglo-Saxon heredity made for political and commercial achievements rather than for artistic attainments.

The Anglo-Saxon has "a fundamental inaptitude for art," declared Fuller. Equally unfortunate for the arts are the American environment, climate, business preoccupations, and the spirit of the age. Fuller concluded that "the world is becoming horrible" and that "art, to-day, is a poor creature who finds herself in a position sadly false; the circumstances of the case make it inevitable that she should cause trouble for herself and for everybody else. . . . Let her, then, retire for a few ages, yielding place to the other concerns and interests that are so much nearer our hearts and so much more in consonance with our requirements. Let us not deplore our inaptitude for art, but let us put a stop to mistaken endeavor and call a halt on misapplied energy."

Even more strongly than his reaction to the Spanish-American War, Fuller's keen disappointment over the "sadly false" position of art in America determined the underlying idea of *The Last Refuge,* the novel which he began in December, 1899, and finished in February, 1900. In the closing days of the century, Fuller worked on his novel in a mood of nostalgic despondency. The America he found most congenial, the America of Longfellow, Norton, and the younger Howells, had already vanished, replaced by an imperialistic America whose center was to be found in booming cities like Chicago and whose horizons were blackened by utility, ugliness, and mediocrity. For Fuller, Europe had once meant escape from materialism and the refreshment of his creative powers, but now he felt that he had had enough of foreign travel. Gloomily, he wrote to Garland, "I guess it's done me all the good it can" (June 22, 1897). Never optimistic and now thoroughly depressed, Fuller knew only too well that on January 9, 1900, he would be forty-three, a middle-aged man; an author whose books were not fulfilling the promise of his youth; and a bachelor obligated to deal with the daily heating, plumbing, and roofing problems of the tenants in his mother's apartments. In such a frame of mind, Fuller worked until *The Last Refuge* became in some respects as much an act of self-criticism as of literary creation.

In *The Last Refuge,* the principal character is Theodor Egmont, Freiherr of Kaltenau, who, on the eve of his fortieth birthday, descends, for the first time in eighteen years, from his ancestral seat in the Vorarlberg into Italy. Rome disappoints him. "Beautiful?" the Freiherr asks himself, "I felt it so, too—once. What would I give to feel it so once more" (2). Hoping to recover the freshness of his own early experiences, the Freiherr accompanies a youth, Bruno de' Brunelli, upon a journey to Sicily to claim his inheritance. Speaking to Bruno, the Freiherr declares, "Your eyes shall be my eyes; your senses shall be my senses. I shall see things as you see them, and feel them as you feel them; and the world that was so beautiful in my youth shall become beautiful once again" (1).

As they journey, they encounter a number of persons, each of whom, for his own particular reason, seeks to find in Sicily his last refuge, the city of La Felice. At the Villa dei Dubbii, just outside La Felice, the City of Happiness, the Freiherr advises all of the principal characters to "leave this place of doubts. Learn once more to trust. The world, we have been taught, is but a reflection of ourselves" (281), and the youthful Bruno adds that the world "is what we make of it. . . . We must take its good and its evil together" (283).

The significance of *The Last Refuge* lies not so much in its message, which is almost a platitude, as in its reflection of Fuller's attitude toward his own career. In phrases that reflect Fuller's self-criticism, the Freiherr reviews the last eighteen years of his life and concludes that it "had been indeed too free;—too free from ties, from duties, from obligations, from restraints; too free from guidance, too free from the kindly pressure of any ordering hand" (5). In the same vein and even more directly applicable to Fuller are the words of the "writer": "I have succeeded . . . I have established myself, and have position, recognition, a following. But my position is only about so high; my recognition not completely general; my following, to confess the truth, rather limited. I ask myself why. I have almost found the answer. My participation in life has been, after all, but partial. I have always felt a slight reluctance about committing myself—a touch of dread about letting myself go" (98-99). Severe as the criticism is, Fuller had identified one of his major problems. Always shy, reserved, his desire for privacy amounting almost to an obsession, Fuller throughout his life had desired to participate only vicariously, or only at a distance, in many of the relationships that most persons enter into easily.

The "writer," however, asserts that to attain the really large following, the universal recognition for which he longs, he himself must participate "in some heart-drama warm with human passion." When the Freiherr protests that he would "feel like an intruder," the "writer" replies that "One *must* intrude. One must gather his data. . . . The tribute due from nature must be exacted" (100-1). In the passage which follows, Fuller defended one of his lifelong attitudes.

> "I understand. The modesty *of* nature must be ruthlessly over-stepped if professional necessities require it. But what I am think-ing of is the tribute of modesty due *to* nature,—the universal freemasonry that should cooperate to cloak charitably the naked-ness of the poor creature taken unaware. I myself try always to have but a dull eye and a deaf ear for any one caught in the open by a great emotional crisis—such a crisis as sets self-mastery beyond reach and puts concealment quite out of the question. Even at the theatre I often find myself wishing for the revival of the Greek masks"—
>
> "You will never make a novelist in the world!"
>
> "I have always suspected that," observed the Freiherr, dryly.

Under the thin disguise of a fictional character, Fuller thus expressed his doubts about his future as a novelist. In his partial participation in life and in his distaste for intruding upon the privacy of others, even in fiction, Fuller recognized an insurmountable barrier to his ever successfully writing the kind of fiction represented by the work of Henry James, Robert Herrick, Frank Norris, and Stephen Crane. In the main, Fuller's doubts were well founded.

From where Fuller stood in 1900, after the publication of *The Last Refuge,* his literary future seemed depressingly bleak. The fiction that had gained him a reputation earlier in the decade, he realized, had been particularly well suited to his abilities because it required neither full participation in life nor the overstepping of the bounds of delicacy, "the modesty due *to* nature." Both *The Chevalier of Pensieri-Vani* and *The Chatelaine of La Trinité* owed their success almost entirely to Fuller's imagination, his skill in rendering the romantic charm of Italy, and the exquisite perfection of his literary style. But the failure of either book to attract a wide audience and the subsequent failure of *The Puppet-Booth* and *From the Other*

Side to win public acclaim led Fuller not only to blame the callousness of the American public to the subtleties of art but also to believe that imagination, romance, and fine writing were going out of fashion. The very slight interest aroused by *The Last Refuge* confirmed him in this opinion.

Fuller might have continued to write in the vein of idealistic travel fiction had not his attitude changed toward Europe, especially toward Italy. Despite his approval of Howells' choice of American subjects for fiction, Europe had always been Fuller's last refuge; but with the Sicilian trip of 1897, he had found it no longer so beautiful, so emotionally satisfying, so creatively refreshing as it had been in his youth. He came back to Chicago, having suddenly realized that Europe could do him no more good, only to recognize in turn that he could never really commit himself fully to Chicago. The sad fact was that he found himself alienated from almost every alternative. His sudden awareness that his two main sources for writing material had turned sour strengthened his doubts about his personal fitness for novel writing. Better than anyone else, Fuller understood with dismay that his career as a novelist had already ended. Not until 1918 would he try again to write a novel, and not until 1924 would he venture to return to Europe. By then the literary procession would have passed him by. The fact is that Fuller made his really significant contribution to American literature in the 1890's; the last thirty years of his life were, in the main, an anticlimax.

CHAPTER 8

Partial Participation

Within a few years after the turn of the century, Fuller had settled into a pattern of living from which he never significantly departed throughout the remainder of his lifetime. Increasingly, he withdrew into himself, kept his movements hidden from his friends, and participated in their lives only upon his own terms. Although friendships became an absolute essential in this vicarious manner of living, and although he liked to play the role of the friendly, helpful "literary uncle," Fuller would permit his friends only the most impersonal and casual knowledge of his own activities. After 1907, Fuller lived frugally in cheap rental houses on the South Side, sometimes remaining at one address only a few days or weeks before moving to another. Either because of his desire to keep his privacy inviolate or perhaps because of his straitened financial circumstances, he never invited any of his friends to visit him.

I A Pattern of Life

In the day-by-day, unrevised entries in his diaries, Hamlin Garland recorded his firsthand observations of Fuller's appearance, the peculiarities of his temperament, and his manner of living. While Fuller was making one of his many visits to the Garlands, Garland wrote in his diary (September 20, 1900) that Fuller "is a joy to us—so quaint—so full of life. He is seeing all that we do and all that we are in his own way. So quaint and bright and keen and incisive." After Fuller had remained for ten days, Garland wrote that he and Zulime "have determined that we cannot live without Henry B. Fuller. He is such a wag—so witty and high spirited in spite of his avowed pessimism." Throughout his diaries, Garland repeatedly emphasized Fuller's outbursts of good humor and the sudden appearances of his characteristic charm.

After 1900, Garland began to notice other, and at times less favorable, traits in Fuller. On January 1, 1901, Garland was describing a small entertainment for a group of artists: "Fuller was there quaint as ever and easily the most interesting of all the men. He was looking worn and haggard. His health is bad and he takes no care of himself at all—especially as to his eating. He remains as remote as ever so far as his actual home-life is concerned. No one calls on him at his home or rooming place—for the reason that we do not feel sure of a welcome. He lives in one little room and without the dignity that should be his." Often, Garland was irritated by Fuller's seedy-looking clothes, the increasing evidences of his eccentricities in small matters, and his habit of "grumbling and groaning and fussing about the house" (Diary, October 12, 1908). In his entry for September 18, 1909, Garland wrote: "Fuller was grouchy and not very vigorous. His censorious habit of mind increases and annoys one. One gets tired of a man who never has anything but 'nippy' words of any book or thing." Garland, however, had no intention of allowing such remarks as these to stand as his judgment of Fuller. When revising this passage of his diary, Garland added, "yet intellectually he is the most distinctive and high-bred individual."

Many of Garland's entries deal with his concern over Fuller's lack of ambition and his generally apathetic outlook. On June 27, 1908, Garland remarked: "Fuller seems not to have any motives left. Nothing interests him any more. He said he only lived in hope of getting away some time to go to Italy and never come back. His attitude is absolutely hopeless. No wife, child or home. He has no real interest—nothing to engage him and he is rapidly degenerating into a funny, slovenly old man."

Although Garland probably overstated the depth of Fuller's pessimism, it is true that on occasion Fuller's mood could be extremely gloomy and that he had virtually abandoned what had been a promising career as a novelist. To conclude, however, that Fuller had no interests is not only to underestimate the extent of Fuller's activities but also to misunderstand Fuller himself. Like the Freiherr in *The Last Refuge*, Fuller was living largely "by proxy," and one indication of his vicarious participation is his eagerness to help Garland with Garland's own literary production, beginning with the initial ideas for books and extending through the final proofreading and the choice of cover designs.

From day to day, Fuller kept himself occupied by regularly visiting his friends, by pursuing an enormous reading program, and by performing literary work that ranged from the composition of short stories to what must be regarded as merely literary hackwork. His intellectual curiosity was phenomenal. In addition to maintaining an active interest in the artistic accomplishments of the painters and sculptors in what he called the "rabbit hutch" of the Fine Arts Building, he spent a great deal of time discussing problems of art and art history with Lorado Taft in his Midway Studios. Fuller also liked to attend lectures at the University of Chicago. Often he passed the entire day reading in the public reading rooms of the Chicago Public Library, particularly the Blackstone Branch, the Newberry Library, and the Crerar scientific library. Hamlin Garland recalled encountering Fuller in the Newberry Library, deeply involved in a study of the size and armament of the navies of the great world powers.[1] Fuller's principal reading material, however, consisted of contemporary literature of all sorts, books relating to Italy, and material about Chicago. In all three areas, Fuller was an expert. Fuller's life was almost wholly intellectual, yet Garland's description of him as "a highly intellectual tramp" (Diary, May 1, 1907), though not meant unkindly, seems hardly just.

II   Art in Satire

Although Fuller had slowed the rate of his literary production, he had not entirely abandoned fiction. In 1901, he brought out *Under the Skylights,* a volume of three novelettes satirizing himself, Hamlin Garland, and the artists of the Little Room who worked "under the skylights" on the topmost floor of the Fine Arts Building. In these stories, which are held together by a general similarity of theme and by repeated use of the same characters, Fuller attained a high level of artistry; and although individual allusions and "hits" have been obscured in the passage of time, the general outlines of Fuller's satirical thrusts continue to be understandable to the modern reader.

In "The Downfall of Abner Joyce," the first novelette in *Under the Skylights,* Abner Joyce (Hamlin Garland), a farm

boy, educated at Flatfield Academy, has achieved literary fame
with his first book, *This Weary World (Main-Travelled Roads)*,
a book of twelve stories featuring the unpleasant aspects of
farm life and advocating populist measures of agrarian reform.
Shortly afterwards, Abner writes a novel, *The Rod of the Op-
pressor (Jason Edwards)*. Both books, grim, rugged, and sincere,
suggest the blunt earnestness and the socially ragged edges of
their author. In his righteous zeal to promote the gospel of
the "Readjusted Tax" (Henry George's Single Tax), Abner
refuses to make the slightest compromise with wealth, gentility,
or luxurious living.

Abner receives an invitation to join the circle of a group
of artists which includes Adrian Bond (Fuller), Medora Giles
(Zulime Taft), and her brother Stephen Giles (Lorado Taft).
Despite Abner's insults and occasional rudeness, the artists
tolerate him; and in the remainder of the story Fuller relates
how Abner succumbs to the charm of the society matron, Mrs.
Potter Pence (possibly Mrs. Potter Palmer) and the attractive
Medora Giles. At the conclusion of the piece, Abner Joyce has
reached "an understanding with the children of Mammon. He—
a great, original genius—had become just like other people.
His downfall was complete" (139).

In the conversations between Adrian Bond and Abner Joyce,
Fuller stated emphatically the difference between his writing and
that of Garland. Advising the "alien romanticist" Bond, Abner,
the veritist, declares that "the way to write about cows in a
pasture is just to write about them—in a simple, straightforward style without any slant toward history or mythology, and
without any cross-references to remote scenes of foreign travel"
(58). Indeed, Abner proclaims that "travel is a mistake" and
that the writer had best "leave the past alone." Bond, speaking
for Fuller, replies, more to himself than to Abner, "I'll stick to
my regular field. . . . Griffins, gorgons, hydras, chimeras dire,
—but no more cows. I was never meant for a veritist."

While underscoring the literary issues which divide his work
from that of Garland, Fuller actually made an apology for his
own position. In a passage that recalls Fuller's early essay
"Howells or James?" Adrian Bond asserts that "I know I ought
to . . . start in to accomplish something more vital, more in-
digenous—less of the marquise and more of the milkmaid . . ."

(41). In the conversational exchange which follows, Fuller exhibited a remarkable insight into his own literary dilemma:

> "Write about the things you know and like," said Abner curtly. . . .
> "If to know and to like were one with me, as they appear to be with you! A boyhood in the country—what a grand beginning! But the things I know are the things I don't like, and the things I like are not always the things I know—oftener the things I feel."

When Abner dismisses Bond as a dilettante who may have some "traces of style" but who lacks "meat," Bond ends the scene by admitting that "clearly the big thing, the sincere thing, the significant thing was beyond his reach."

Fuller had thought about these issues throughout his career. He could see the force of the arguments advanced by the realists or veritists who urged the American writer to deal with the American local scene "in a simple, straightforward style." For Fuller, the local scene would mean Chicago and all that was implied by *The City's Maw,* the title of the novel that Bond refused to write. But Fuller saw that for him to write in this vein would be for him to deal with the ordinary, the commonplace, even the repulsive and to become a reporter not a writer (Abner refers to the artist as "the reporter sublimated"). Worst of all, Fuller would have to abandon his concept of literature as the creation of beauty by the exercise of the imagination. Fuller had made his decision, and in his declaration that *"The City's Maw* must remain unwritten" (42), "The Downfall of Abner Joyce" becomes more a defense of Fuller's own literary position than a caricature of Hamlin Garland.

Although the portrait of Hamlin Garland as Abner Joyce was not flattering, Garland probably recognized the essential truth of what Fuller wrote and never allowed the work to diminish their friendship. In his diaries and in his volumes of autobiography, Garland said nothing about Abner Joyce. On the other hand, Garland recorded his immense delight over both of the other stories in *Under the Skylights.* On December 29, 1900, when Fuller read "Dr. Gowdy and the Squash" to the Garlands and the Tafts, Garland wrote in his diary, "it is a capital satire—just the right tone, and hit off all conditions here most happily. It had a little of me—a good deal of the Central Art

Association, the Institute, and also a good deal of himself." On February 5, 1901, when Fuller read "Little O'Grady vs. the Grindstone," Garland called it "a delicious piece of satirical comedy based on an actual happening here. . . . Fuller was at his best and chuckled with us over the hits of the story. His delight in it was as great as ours."

"Little O'Grady vs. the Grindstone," the second story in *Under the Skylights,* satirizes the businessman's approach to art as well as the competition and intrigue among artists in Chicago. The directors of the Grindstone National Bank, which is experiencing financial difficulties because of its heavy investment in the failing Pin-and-Needle Combine expect to spend twenty-five thousand dollars for the art work on the front of their new building. Their motives are expressed forcefully by one of the directors who exclaims, "To hell with art! What I wanted to do was to advertise my business" (289). Angered by their contempt for art and the artists who have endeavored to please them, little Terence O'Grady, a sculptor from the Rabbit-Hutch, denounces the bankers for their lack of culture and public spirit. Meanwhile, the artists seek to advance their interests by intriguing with society leaders like Mrs. Potter Pence and wealthy depositors to obtain the commission. The bank fails before any decision about the art work can be reached. Fuller is critical of both groups. Unfortunately, his satire, which he thought the best of the three pieces in the volume, has been blunted by the passing of time.

In "Dr. Gowdy and the Squash," which still retains most of its original sparkle, Fuller ridiculed those who believed that "the hope of American art is in the West, and that the best thing we can do is to paint the familiar things of daily life" (336). Dr. William S. Gowdy (whose career and opinions resemble those of the Reverend Frank Wakely Gunsaulus) is a minister who habitually enlivens his sermons with references to art. Dr. Gowdy, a trustee of the Art Academy and the author of *Onward and Upward,* believes strongly that nothing "was more calculated to ennoble and refine human nature than the practice of art itself" (328).

Dr. Gowdy's book fires the ambition of Jared Stiles, a young country bumpkin who is already a failure at farming, to learn to paint. Encouraged by the Western Art Circuit (the Chicago

Central Art Association), which was sponsored by Abner Joyce, Adrian Bond, and Stephen Giles, Jared selects the squash as his subject. Soon Jared's squash paintings become famous; the newspapers describe him as "The Western Angelus," and editorial writers contrast "the sturdy and wholesome truthfulness of his genius with the vain imaginings of so-called idealists" (356). Only Dr. Gowdy dislikes Jared's paintings. The minister keeps Jared's work out of the Art Academy and from his pulpit delivers an impassioned sermon against the rural artist; but Dr. Gowdy cannot maintain his opposition single-handedly. Faced with opposition from wealthy members of his congregation who have purchased the squash paintings, the possible loss of his place on the board of trustees of the Art Academy, and the force of Jared's own personality, Dr. Gowdy makes his peace with the squash painter.

Beneath the comedy and the witticism of the three novelettes in *Under the Skylights,* Fuller was seriously defending his own artistic creed. Below his surface playfulness lay the whole long history of Fuller's quarrel with Chicago, his disappointment over the "upward movement," and his growing conviction that he was fighting a losing battle in defense of romance, idealism, and imagination as the essentials of art. If the art of the novelist was to become in the future merely the act of reporting, Fuller would withdraw from competition. His decision to withdraw becomes the salient fact of his career after 1900.

III   The Silent Years

During the fifteen years following publication of *Under the Skylights,* Fuller made no effort to write either novels or additional novelettes. In a letter to William Dean Howells dated April 16, 1909, Fuller declared that "repugnance toward writing further fiction is now my normal state." Of Fuller's apathy during these years, Hamlin Garland's diaries furnish abundant, firsthand evidence. Garland's entries contain repeated references to Fuller's lack of motive for writing, his abandonment of the novel form, and his pessimistic outlook. On one occasion, when Fuller arrived to spend the summer, Garland wrote, "Fuller came in and brought his trunks. . . . He gets more and more eccentric. I heard him talking to himself as he worked about his room. Just a pleasant running commentary on what he was doing and thinking. He has nothing to do now but trip from one friend to the next—a sheer waste of genius" (Diary, July 1, 1912).

At intervals, Fuller engaged in writing short pieces suitable for editorials and newspaper columns. For this kind of writing, he was eminently qualified by virtue of his wide reading, his expert knowledge of Chicago, and his vast fund of general information about architecture, sculpture, and literature. During 1900, a series of his editorials appeared in *The Saturday Evening Post*;[2] and beginning with an article about Gabriele D'Annunzio's *Il Fuoco* on June 9, followed on July 14 by an essay entitled "Civic Federation and Literature," Fuller became a contributor to the Chicago *Post*. During the following year, Fuller contributed to the paper, now known as the Chicago *Evening Post,* on a regular basis, writing a column for each Saturday's issue during the months of April through September. Generally, Fuller wrote about Chicago; American and European literature; and, less frequently, opera, sculpture, and painting.

From April 19, 1902, to March 28, 1903, Fuller actually took charge of the weekly literary supplement of the Chicago *Evening Post*. For each issue, he contributed a review or a column of general interest. In the forty-six articles which he wrote, Fuller discussed the work of such writers as Henry James, F. Marion Crawford, Edith Wharton, Frank Norris, William Dean Howells, Jack London, Robert Louis Stevenson, Mrs. Humphry Ward, and the leading contemporary Italian and Russian novelists. His articles about general literary subjects included such titles as "Erroneous Ideas about Prospects for the 'Great American Novel,' " "Is Great Literature of the Future to Come from American Continent?" "Increase in American Fiction of Aristocratic Social Ideals," and "Are Publishers Unjust to Young and Unknown Authors?"[3]

Again, in 1910, Fuller resorted to literary journalism. This time he contributed short pieces, most of them editorials, to the Chicago *Record Herald*. Shortly after he began, Garland noted in his diary that Fuller's outlook was improving and that the routine demanded by the work had proved particularly beneficial to him. In a spurt of activity, Fuller wrote fifteen hundred editorials in 1910-11 and about four hundred in 1913-14.[4] Although most of them are unsigned, the few pieces which bear his name and which may be regarded as typical of the others deal with general subjects only tangentially related to literature.

Upon the seventy-odd pieces that he wrote between 1900 and 1903 for the Chicago *Evening Post* and the huge number that he produced between 1910 and 1914 for the Chicago *Record Herald,* Fuller lavished the same meticulous care in preparation and writing that in the past he had devoted to the composition of his novels; yet, except for a very small monetary reward and the slight advantage of regular publication, he gained little benefit from this hackwork. More than anything else, these ventures into literary journalism furnish additional evidence of his retreat from the center to the peripheral areas of literature and his compelling need to keep himself occupied.

From time to time, during these years, Fuller wrote short stories, but his average rate of production was less than one story each year. In 1908, he gathered together four of his stories which had already appeared in *Scribner's* and in *The Century Magazine,* added to the group three new stories, and published the collection as *Waldo Trench and Others: Stories of Americans in Italy.*

As the subtitle implies, the seven stories are linked by the general theme of the American sojourner in such Italian cities as Rome, Florence, Venice, and Palermo. Immediately, reviewers called attention to the similarity between Fuller's work and that of Henry James. Because of the subject matter, the style, and, in several instances, the plot, Fuller's volume invited the comparison with James. "Eliza Hepburn's Deliverance," for example, was described as a "Fullerized 'Europe,' " while "A Coal from the Embers" was considered reminiscent of James's "The Aspern Papers."[5] No one, however, regarded Fuller as either an imitator or as a follower of James.

While praising Fuller's technical skill in story-telling, his subtle stylistic effects, and his delicate humor, critics generally failed to notice the undercurrent of anti-American criticism in Fuller's work. He had taken a mildly critical attitude in his earlier European fiction; but in these pieces, written after the Spanish-American War, there was an edge to his remarks that was sharper than it had been in his previous work. In "New Wine," for example, Fuller underscored his habitual distrust of American superiority and of American willingness to meddle in other people's affairs. In this piece, an Italian nobleman, attracted to a young American girl, meets disaster when he applies American precepts to the Italian peasants on his estate. Fuller's criticism of the war with Spain lies behind the remark made to the Italian by Bannister Grayle, a wealthy young American tourist: "If the Americans admire a man who can humbug, how much more do they admire a man who can plunder!" (80-81). Even more pointedly, Miss Sibyl McChesney affirms that the Italian peasants "merely ask that the car of Juggernaut shall roll over them. . . . Well, gratify them. Roll" (88).

American snobbery, crudity, and naïveté appear throughout the stories. In "For the Faith," Philippa, a young instructor at a Connecticut academy, endeavors to absorb European culture in a few weeks' tour. Asked what she is trying to accomplish, Philippa replies: "I was trying to help America become the greatest ever. We need culture, and I was doing my best to cultivate myself, and to aid those who depend on me for instruction and guidance" (189). In "Addolorata's Intervention," Fuller satirizes young Miss Addie Matthews, who is "more cultivated than Culture in Culture's most cultivated moments" (276). Although Miss Matthews has become "so completely Italianate as to call herself 'Addolorata' " (276), she admits that "with every passing day I come to feel surer that, after all, I still view the great fundamentals through the atmosphere of my native Poughkeepsie" (293). Similar examples of Americans searching for culture in a Europe that they cannot, or will not, understand because American values oppose the fundamentals of humanistic culture may be found in the other stories in the volume.

The deep undercurrent of satire on the American tourist, however, is perhaps best seen in the title story, "Waldo Trench Regains His Youth." On board the *Macedonia*, a ship filled with Americans taking "guided tours" of Italy, Waldo Trench, a young man originally from Stapleville, Nebraska, but lately from Oklahoma, meets three other Americans also bound for Italy: Aurelius Gilmore, the narrator; Elizabeth Payne, a young woman in search of "Culture"; and Mrs. Madeline K. Pritchard, her aunt. All of the characters, except Mrs. Pritchard, a middle-aged woman from "near Cleveland," are going to Italy for "improvement." Having been around the world twice and having spent the years of her youth in the mad pursuit of culture, Mrs. Pritchard has now "accomplished the grand circle" and has reached the point "where culture, as a moving force, was genially ignored" (8). She is "reverting" to the present. She prefers her own "dialect" to correct grammar, the hand organ to a symphony, a French automobile show to an Italian painting gallery, and her own taste in contemporary furniture to that approved by *House Beautiful*. In sum, Mrs. Pritchard now lives in the present and enjoys her anti-cultural sentiments. She is one of Fuller's most lively and humorous characters.

The emphasis of Fuller's story, however, falls on Waldo Trench. In contrast to Mrs. Pritchard's attitude, Waldo Trench values the past. For him, antiquity is the only criterion of artistic merit; and, as he hastens from period to period, backward in time, he finally reaches the Etruscans. He becomes excited about old Etruscan foundations (the walls have long since crumbled) until he encounters an Englishman who super-ciliously dismisses the Etruscans with the retort, "I'm after the Pelasgians" (40). When Trench learns that the Pelasgians are older than the Etruscans, he declares, "Then I've got to take them up right away" (40). Before Waldo can completely lose himself in the prehistoric past, he discovers his love for Miss Payne and they resolve to "remain modern."

In view of the admiration for the monuments of Etruscan culture that Fuller had voiced at the outset of his career in *The Chevalier of Pensieri-Vani*, his faintly contemptuous attitude in "Waldo Trench Regains His Youth" must be understood as a reflection of Fuller's changed attitude toward Europe. At fifty, as he conceived the character of Waldo Trench, Fuller may have felt that his own veneration for the past had restricted his full participation in life around him. Speaking through Mrs. Pritchard, Fuller's advice to young Waldo Trench was to forget the mysteries of prehistoric antiquities and instead to use his vigor, energy, and singleness of purpose in Oklahoma. At any event, Fuller was certain that—regardless of his own case—this course was the best one for Americans to pursue.

[*143*]

Literary journalism and the occasional composition of short stories were not the only literary activities which engaged Fuller's time during the years before America entered World War I. In 1912, Harriet Monroe, then about to found her remarkable and influential *Poetry: A Magazine of Verse,* invited Fuller to become the first member of its advisory committee. As a writer respected everywhere for his high standards of craftsmanship and his profound grasp of artistic principles, Fuller's name was an asset. Aware he had written no poetry, Miss Monroe believed, as she later wrote, that "he had a poet's imagination and keen feeling for rhythm, and beauty of style."[6] Although Fuller helped her to discover new talent and to establish the progressive, even revolutionary, reputation of the magazine, his most sustained contribution lay in his editorial abilities. As Hamlin Garland, Hobart Chatfield-Taylor, Lorado Taft, and many others could affirm, Fuller was an editor and proofreader without equal. Much of the excellence of *Poetry* was due to Fuller's high standards of writing and printing.

IV A New Beginning

In 1916, after ten years of silence, Fuller's interest in writing suddenly revived. "I am doing a set of 20-25 *vers libre* biographies for a book—each piece about 160-170 lines; many of them condensed short stories, in pseudo-poetic guise," he announced to an astonished Hamlin Garland (January 14, 1916). "They touch miscellaneously on art, literature, stage, politics, society, sociology, psychies, morals, et cetry," continued Fuller; "I feel that I am escaping the multifarious deadening detail of the conventional short story."

As his comments imply, Fuller was trying to adapt the free-verse form used by Edgar Lee Masters in *Spoon River Anthology* to the writing of short stories. Fuller believed, as he wrote in *The Dial* (December 14, 1916), that the contemporary American short story had become a "mass of deadwood," written by formula and hamstrung by conventions of description, characterization, and action. In its place, Fuller wished to substitute "the short story written in free verse," which, he argued, could be biographical, episodical, or semi-lyrical. Balancing "on the fence between poetry and prose," asserted Fuller, the free-verse short story "can give in a single epithet the essence of a prose sentence, and in a single phrase the spirit of a prose paragraph."

Within three months, Fuller had written twenty-five verse stories, most of them biographies, and was trying to place them for publication. Harriet Monroe accepted two for *Poetry,* Francis Hackett took two for *The New Republic,* and Houghton Mifflin Company agreed to publish all of them in a single volume. Edgar Lee Masters encouraged Fuller's experiment and helped to read the page proof of the book.

Early in February, 1917, Fuller's twenty-five free-verse experiments were published as *Lines Long and Short.* Virtually all of the pieces are biographies, Fuller's preference, numerically at least, being slightly in favor of men over women. Although Fuller's tone was friendly, informal, even conversational, his customary playfulness and humor were lacking; instead, he sounded a pervasive note of sadness and futility. Almost invariably, youth appears as a time for activity, optimism, and adventure; middle-age follows as a period in which youthful hopes fade, disappointments multiply, and marriages crumble; and by sixty, the subject has either died in the knowledge of his failure or faces an empty, lonely old age. The monotony which results from this uniform pattern of ideas constitutes one of the principal weaknesses of Fuller's biographies.

The general content of Fuller's verse biographies, as well as their frequently close relationship to his own life, may be seen from the selections entitled "Tobias Holt, Bachelor" (the first piece in the volume) and "Postponement." At twenty, Tobias Holt displays the same interest in young ladies as the other men of his circle. At twenty-eight, he is still single. In his thirties, he often dines with his married friends and sends presents to their children; but, as he approaches fifty, he finds that "Uncle Toby" must send more presents, learn more humorous stories, and lend more books than ever before to insure his continued welcome. At sixty-five, he is keeping busy but finding his life "rather bleak" as he lies ill in a boardinghouse. Holt's vicarious living and his partial participation in life suggest Fuller himself. Significantly, Fuller refused to write the ending, but affirmed that "it's sad to be old, and alone."

Fuller's use of his own life for his verse biographies becomes almost painfully apparent in "Postponement." Except for the fact that the subject of this piece never visits Europe, the relationship between Albert F. McComb and Henry B. Fuller appears remarkably close. At seventeen, after reading about Dickens' London, Ruskin's Venice, and the Italy of Raphael, Albert dedicates himself to the romance of the past in faraway places. At twenty-one, he takes a "position," but his heart is never in the business. At twenty-five, he refuses a share in the business for fear entanglements may prevent him from "crossing over" once he has saved enough money; and for the same reason, at twenty-six, he refuses marriage. While others make fortunes in the West, Albert lives mainly in the Italy of his imagination. At fifty-two, he finds he must help his grandnieces with the grocery bills. Finally, "past sixty," when he suddenly inherits the money to cross over, the war prevents him from going. Albert retires, his eyes now "too dim to see the Here and Now, | Or to divine the local glories Just About to Be." Thus, the events of Albert's life seem to justify the comment of the few persons who remark upon his death at "sixty-odd," the comment with which Fuller prefaced the verse biography:

> That he had lived a futile life,
> And that Europe was to blame:
> His continual hankering after the Old World
> Had made him a failure in the New.

Incidents from Fuller's own life, as well as many of his characteristic attitudes, may be found throughout the verse biographies. His antagonism to marriage, for example, appears in "Rigmarole," "Victory," "The Statue," "The Outsider," and "Chameleon." His views on single life provide material for "Polly Greene," "Death of Aunt Juliana," and "Tobias Holt, Bachelor." His criticism of the emptiness of business life finds expression in "Aridity," "Toward Childhood," "Manners," and "The Day of Danger." Other sketches, such as "The Two Apprentices," "Alonzo Grout," "The Art of Life," and "Deliquescence," reflect the unhappiness and frustrations of the artist in America. Consistently, in *Lines Long and Short,* the characters are defeated men and women who have failed either to realize their potential or to achieve happiness in the fields of their choice.

Both the merit and the weakness of Fuller's volume lie in his compression of material for a lengthy story into the space of a few hundred lines of verse. At his best in sketches like "Tobias Holt, Bachelor" and "Postponement," Fuller developed convincingly a single aspect of a subject's life within remarkably few lines. On the whole, however, Fuller's free-verse biographies suffer more than they gain from the compression necessitated by the form. For brevity, Fuller sacrificed the details of character and incident that would carry intellectual and emotional conviction to the reader. Probably, Fuller demanded too much from the form. Had he related his individual pieces, as Masters had done in *Spoon River Anthology,* or as Sherwood Anderson was to do in *Winesburg, Ohio,* Fuller might have been more successful. As it is, *Lines Long and Short* remains a collection of separate, free-verse biographies possessing no essential organic unity.

In July, 1917, only six months after *Lines Long and Short* was published, Fuller completed *On the Stairs,* his first novel in eighteen years. The two books are related both in theory and in content. *Lines Long and Short* had been an effort to compress the short story form; in *On the Stairs,* Fuller attempted to compress the novel. Explaining his theory in an article entitled "A Plea for Shorter Novels," which appeared in *The Dial* (August 30, 1917), Fuller declared that "compressed form is itself one of the manifestations of force—an evidence of vigor." The novelist, asserted Fuller, should be able to express himself adequately in fifty thousand words instead of ninety thousand which were required by the novel usually considered of "moderate length." Fuller intended *On the Stairs* to be an illustration of this principle.

The relationship between *Lines Long and Short* and *On the Stairs* extends beyond the form to the content. Despite the separate identities of the verse biographies, the lives of Fuller's characters may be separated into two distinct patterns: the subject whose career, in his alienation from Chicago, suggests that of Fuller himself; and the person who conforms without serious questioning to what the community expects of him. In *Lines Long and Short,* both avenues of development result in unhappiness. In many respects, *On the Stairs* is a longer, more poignant exposition of a similar theme.

With respect to construction and the symmetry of its design, *On the Stairs* approaches artistic perfection more nearly than any other novel by Fuller. The action takes place within an envelope of two incidents, both recounted in the opening pages. In 1873, Johnny McComas stands aside as Raymond Prince descends the main stairs of Grant's Private Academy. In 1916, Raymond Prince stands aside as Johnny McComas descends the marble stairway of the Mid-Continent National Bank. On both occasions, they exchange the same words of greeting. Fuller's objective in the remainder of the novel is to account for the reversal of their roles.

Raymond Prince, whose life resembles that of Fuller himself, represents the third generation of the family. His grandfather, Jehiel Prince, of New England ancestry, had founded the family fortunes; but in the hands of his son, James Prince, they had diminished rather than increased. Of the three men, Raymond is least capable, either by inclination or by temperament, of restoring the position of the Prince family in society. Raymond, in fact, develops a settled repugnance to business; instead, he devotes his life to music, literature, painting, and foreign travel. At fifty, having divorced his wife, he abandons his esthetic concerns and tries to recoup his financial affairs, only to recognize how totally unfit he is to compete in business enterprises. Forced to sell his house at a loss, Raymond moves into a bachelor's den in a private hotel. A lonely figure, no longer participating actively in life, he lives mainly in his memories of his European experiences, subscribes to a branch of the public library, and occasionally visits picture exhibitions or attends musical concerts.

In almost every respect a sharp contrast to Raymond's ineffectual participation in the life of the city, the career of Johnny McComas seems remarkably successful. As Raymond moves downhill, Johnny rises from rags to riches. Beginning life in the stable behind the Prince mansion, Johnny becomes a crude but gregarious "go-getter." He cares nothing for books or art; he lacks taste, refinement, and sensibility; but he possesses both the ability and the ambition to make money. After marrying a rich man's daughter, Johnny takes advantage of his father-in-law's capital to strengthen the financial position of his bank, shrewdly concludes several lucrative "deals," and obtains private "tips" before investing his money in stocks. In every respect, Johnny conforms to the money-based standards of Chicago.

Eventually, Johnny marries Raymond's former wife and adopts his son Albert. When Albert, in the final scene of the novel, marries Johnny's daughter by his first marriage, Raymond Prince has become "an unregarded and negligible spectator" (265) in one of the back pews of the church.

Outwardly, at least, Johnny McComas, the crude, raw, vigorous force, wins everything, while Raymond Prince, the sensitive, cultured intellectual, declines, without even making a fight, to the level of vicarious participation, a passive "onlooker in life" (250). Though Fuller has refined his characterization, made Johnny hard but attractive through his activity, Johnny's affinities are yet with the "cliff-dwellers" and the moneymakers. For all his gregariousness, Johnny has no real perception of the values of life, no worthwhile goal for his activity, and no desire to resist the pressures for conformity. His material prosperity and his ceaseless activity are achieved at the cost of the human spirit.

The major weakness of Fuller's novel, however, lies in the fact that, instead of opposing the market-place values of Johnny with a positive assertion of the worth of humanistic pursuits, Fuller deliberately made them lead to a life equally as futile as that of Johnny McComas. Raymond's lifelong interest in all of the arts leads eventually to the negation of the very humanistic spirit which culture is supposed to foster. In place of a "paradise within," Raymond creates his own private hell of loneliness, futility, and hopelessness. In the end, Fuller stacked the cards against his own case and wrote his own sense of failure into his fictional character. Reading *On the Stairs,* Hamlin Garland recognized what Fuller had done. "Henry B.'s book came in today," wrote Garland in his diary (March 30, 1918), "and I read it at a sitting but it left a gray desolation in my spirit. What's the use?"

In writing *On the Stairs,* Fuller had broken his long silence primarily to restate his case against Chicago and, beyond Chicago, America; but in the thirty-five years separating *The Cliff-Dwellers* and *On the Stairs,* Fuller's attitude had not changed greatly. In 1917, he still believed that the values of the market-place were essentially false values and that the individual could best realize his potential as a human being through travel and an understanding of the several arts. The fact remains, however, that there is virtually nothing in *On the Stairs* that Fuller had not already written and written more forcefully during the decade of the 1890's.

In both *Lines Long and Short* and *On the Stairs,* Fuller had been experimenting with new fictional techniques. In *Bertram Cope's Year,* his next novel, Fuller's choice of homosexuality as his subject matter was an experiment that amounted almost to a sensation. To be sure, he had earlier glanced at it in "At Saint Judas's," one of the dramatic pieces in *The Puppet-Booth,* but his treatment had been neither explicit nor extensive. Despite the comparative freedom to deal with sexual relationships which had recently been won for the novel by such writers as Theodore Dreiser, Stephen Crane, and Frank Norris, homosexuality as primary subject matter for a novel had occurred so rarely in American fiction as to be virtually unknown. Moreover, in view of Fuller's long-standing aversion to the slightest hint of indelicacy in fiction—an aversion which colored his distaste for naturalistic fiction—his choice of the homosexual theme becomes very remarkable.

The plot of *Bertram Cope's Year* is developed with Fuller's usual care for the architectonics of fiction. As the novel opens, Bertram Cope, a young instructor at a small college in Wisconsin, has left behind his intimate friend, Arthur Lemoyne, to return to the university at Churchton for graduate study. Cope quickly enters the social circle of Mrs. Medora Phillips, a widow, whose house shelters, in addition to herself and her late husband's half-brother Joseph Foster, three artistically minded young women—Amy Leffingwell, Hortense Dunton, and Carolyn Thorpe. Mrs. Phillips also includes among her select friends Basil Randolph, described by Fuller as a graying "scholar *manqué*," who, though not an alumnus himself, likes to participate vicariously in academic life and who "would have enjoyed knowing, and knowing intimately" (13), a few select young men at the institution.

Bertram Cope rapidly becomes the object of the attentions of all the leading characters. For a time, Amy Leffingwell traps him into an engagement from which he scarcely escapes before he becomes entangled, successively, by Hortense Dunton and Carolyn Thorpe. Although Cope remains cold and indifferent to the advances of all the women, he responds warmly to both

Arthur Lemoyne and to Basil Randolph. To obtain room to entertain Cope on weekends, Randolph moves to a larger apartment; but Randolph proves no match for his younger rival, Arthur Lemoyne. At Cope's insistence, Lemoyne comes to the university and immediately asserts his claim to Cope's affections. Unfortunately, Lemoyne, after playing the part of a girl in a campus play, makes suggestive gestures toward another male student, an act which brings about his dismissal. Cope leaves the university with him; and, after the two young men spend several days together Cope implies in a letter to Mrs. Phillips that they have gone their separate ways.

Bertram Cope's Year is an unsuccessful novel. Its fatal weakness lies not so much in Fuller's choice of homosexuality for his subject matter as in his failure to deal adequately with the impact of sexual abnormality upon the lives of his characters. Although he supplied abundant evidence of the homosexual tendencies of all the major male characters, he never once indicated the tension or the emotional conflicts which accompany or result from their sexual deviations. To have probed the inner psychological problems of his characters would, of course, have violated Fuller's sense of delicacy; but his failure to deal with this aspect of his subject makes the introduction of the material rather pointless and the novel more sensational than meaningful.

After finishing *Bertram Cope's Year* in May, 1918, Fuller negotiated with several New York firms for its publication; but, probably because of its subject, he could not reach agreement with any of them. Eventually, his friend, Ralph Seymour, who printed *Poetry,* brought out the novel as a favor to Fuller. When it appeared in October, 1919, very few copies were sold; and it was generally ignored in the periodical press. Sometime later, Fuller collected the unbound sheets from Seymour and destroyed them.

V   The Last Years

Between 1917 and 1919, Fuller had published three books, none of which, from his point of view, had been successful. Friendly critics had praised his experiments in *Lines Long and Short* and *On the Stairs,* but *Bertram Cope's Year* had encountered either mild hostility or silence. Once again, Fuller retired from the field. "My disrelish for the writing-and-publishing game," wrote Fuller to Garland (May 22, 1920), "is now absolute. There seems to be no way for one to get read or paid, so—Shutters up."

So far as writing novels was concerned, Fuller kept the shutters up until the last few months before his death in 1929; yet, even though he was aware that his major work had been completed with the publication of *Bertram Cope's Year*, Fuller by no means withdrew from literary affairs. His knowledge of the history of artistic movements in Illinois, particularly Chicago, brought him in 1920 an invitation to write two chapters in *The Centennial History* of Illinois; and Fuller's contributions to the multi-volume historical survey, "Development of Arts and Letters" and "The Growth of Education, Art, and Letters," were widely acknowledged as authoritative.[7]

In the years following, Fuller read first manuscript and then page proof for the still publishing Hobart Chatfield-Taylor, Lorado Taft, and Hamlin Garland, in whose literary autobiographies Fuller's name appears repeatedly. He limited his own writing to the composition of literary articles for a number of prominent journals. A list of the periodicals for which Fuller wrote would include *The Freeman, The New Republic, The Nation, The Bookman, Commonweal, Poetry, Saturday Review of Literature,* and *Literary Digest International Book Review.* In addition, Fuller contributed articles for the literary sections of the Chicago *Tribune,* the New York *Times,* the New York *Evening Post,* and the New York *Herald-Tribune.*

The majority of Fuller's articles for these periodicals may scarcely be called hackwork. Beginning with his reviews for *The Dial,* which he wrote between 1917 and 1919, Fuller's incisive analysis and thoughtful criticism of literature and art, mostly non-fiction, generally determined the editorial attitude of the journal for which he was writing. Particularly in *The Freeman* was Fuller's commentary influential. His articles about James Branch Cabell, Giles Lytton Strachey, Preserved Smith, Percy Lubbock, Henry James, and Hamlin Garland were widely admired and acknowledged as authoritative expressions of conservative literary opinion.[8] His prominence as a nationally known reviewer brought his own work to the attention of such men as Carl Van Vechten, Van Wyck Brooks, Francis Hackett, H. L. Mencken, and Carl Van Doren. To his amusement and immense satisfaction, Fuller found himself in the position of being almost "revived" as a novelist at the very time that he had abandoned the writing of novels.

In the spring of 1924, Fuller proudly noted that in the past year he had written sixty articles, reviews, and short stories. Financed in part by this writing and in part by the maturing of a thousand-dollar bond, Fuller, now sixty-seven and not in the best of health, determined to make one more visit to Europe before settling down, as he wrote Garland late in March, "for the finish." In a fashion reminiscent of the Freiherr's journey through Italy with young Bruno in *The Last Refuge,* Fuller planned to make the trip with William Emery Shepherd, a senior at the University of Illinois. At twenty-two, Shepherd was, as Fuller pointed out, the same age as he had been when he made his first European tour. Through March and April, as Fuller mapped their itinerary with his usual thoroughness, there were moments when he felt he really did not wish to make the journey. As late as May 1, replying to Garland's own doubts about wanting to visit London, Fuller noted that "off and on, I feel that way myself—sort of wishing, every few days, that I wasn't going, after all."

Early in June, after several days' sightseeing in New York, Fuller and Shepherd sailed for England. In London, they met Hamlin Garland, a solitary sightseer, eager for Fuller's companionship. Garland thought his old friend looked tired and ready to "quit and go home if he could decently do so."⁹ After spending several weeks in England, Fuller and Shepherd remained in Paris for ten days, then travelled through Switzerland down into Italy. "My boy is not learning travel," wrote Fuller, August 9, from Venice. "Travel is a chore," he continued, "a job, almost a cross; and you were well advised to keep to the comforts and conveniences of London."

After his European tour in 1924, Fuller's output of articles declined. Much of his time was occupied with visits to the Garlands and other friends, the proof-reading of his friends' manuscripts, and discussions of literary matters. In the evenings, he liked to play dominoes or "hearts" with the Garland family. In the summer of 1926, Garland doubted that Fuller would ever write much more; but he affirmed that Fuller, whose hair and beard had long since turned white, was still the most satisfactory companion of his old age.[10] In a letter to Garland, January 1, 1927, from Chicago, Fuller wrote that he was "beginning New Year's at a new address—no damn Kitchenetters swarming on all hands." Fuller's reference was to a rooming house on Harper Avenue, the last of a long succession of rooming houses in which he had lived during the past three decades. Here, by himself, as he wished, Fuller lived the remaining two years of his life; and, here, to the vast astonishment of his friends, he wrote two more novels and even began a third before the heart attack that ended his life.

On his seventy-second birthday, January 9, 1929, after a silence of ten years, Fuller was once more writing a novel. On January 14, he wrote Garland:

> Did I mention a book? Well, there is one; so far along now, that I feel quite sure of it. Wheeled in on Dec. 30, and have written 27,000 words (twice over—well typewritten) in sixteen days; fourteen chaps.—there may be 20-22. I'm sorry to say, however, that the book is of a type you won't care for: a travel-fiction *de fantaisie,* centering about the Mediterranean, and taking in everything from the Alps to the Sahara. I have taken some of the Characters from my early Italian books for the "stock" of the soup and have added new, present-day types for every spoonful—folks of all varieties and of all nationalities. It all seems to come very easily, as you may judge—right of the air; but whether it will find a publisher is another *question*—and I can't afford to print another book at my own expense.

Before the end of January, Fuller had finished his novel, entitled *Gardens of This World,* sent the manuscript to a publisher, and begun a second novel.

At intervals, Fuller kept Garland informed of his progress. By the beginning of April, Fuller had written two-thirds of the new volume which he was to call *Not on the Screen;* and by the end of May, Alfred A. Knopf had issued contracts for both books. "Life for Henry, you see," he wrote Garland on May 25, "is getting down to a matter of credit: he wants to finish up not only emphatically but *well.* To add to the emphasis, if not to the well-ness, he is now in his third book, having written the first chapter." In the same letter, he added, "I've never felt more write-y nor had a better run of ideas (am just *ailing enough* to make them come!)."

The theme of *Gardens of This World* arises from Fuller's belief that there are places where for a moment at least the sensitive individual may effectively shut out of his life "the ugly, the banal, the wide wastes of horror" (3). To discover these gardens, the Chevalier of Pensieri-Vani and the Seigneur of Hors-Concours, now old men, begin a journey in Paris. Their quest leads them through France, Spain, Morocco, along the shores of the Mediterranean, Italy, and back again to Paris. Each of the twenty-four chapters of the novel contains a separate episode which may conceivably relate to the principal theme; but, as the novel progresses, the gardens motif becomes secondary to the individual incidents. Indeed, after the early chapters, only the reappearance of the same characters provides the book with a semblance of unity.

Fuller enjoyed bringing back to fictional life the characters who had been admired in his early "idealistic travel-fiction." His readers, who remembered *The Chevalier of Pensieri-Vani, The Chatelaine of La Trinité,* and *The Last Refuge,* reencountered all the important figures, and many of the minor characters, in *Gardens of this World.* In addition to the Chevalier and Hors-Concours, those whom Fuller revived included the Chatelaine of La Trinité, now the head of a Protestant sisterhood in Lausanne; Aurelia West, now Madame la Comtesse Aurélia de Feuillevolante, of Paris; Tempo-Rubato, now the Duke of Largo; and the Freiherr von Kaltenau. The Prorege of Arcopia, the Duke of Avon and Severn, and George W. Occident have died; but, in part, at least, their places have been taken by the Duke's nephew, who has succeeded to the title, and by Occident's son, an aviator.

Although Fuller tried once again to evoke the charm of Europe that he had conveyed effectively to American readers in his early work, he was only partly successful. In the Freiherr's farewell to Italy, the reader finds a trace of Fuller's earlier, romantic style: "Never had cypresses seemed deeper, denser, more heavily burdened with the centuries. Never had closer shadows been thrown; never had a white town, an azure lake, a purpling headland behind it, shown through aged trunks with a greater intensity of charm" (151-52). Such passages as this one are, however, exceptional. On the whole, Fuller did not succeed in conveying the charm of these gardens because they no longer held a charm for him. Instead of the romantic glow of the Italian countryside that he had rendered convincingly in *The Chevalier of Pensieri-Vani,* Fuller constructed in *Gardens of This World* a novel whose characters move across a bright, gleaming surface that is polished but lacks depth.

In one of his last letters to Garland (June 10, 1929), Fuller remarked that he had written *Gardens of This World* to please himself but that *Not on the Screen* was very much a different matter. "It's Chicago to-day," declared Fuller. "Clubs, opera, football, teas, prize-fights, art-exhibits, kept women, private fisticuffs, police, bathing parties, 'orgies,' etc. etc. That is to say, it's a *righthanded* version of a lefthanded 'film' society-story. Fun to do—and it means something. It's got sense."

As his comments about the work implied, Fuller intended *Not on the Screen* to show how a novelist using the technique of realism would develop a plot which in the motion pictures had been melodrama. As the novel opens, a young couple, Embert Howell and Evelyn Trent, are watching a motion picture. On the screen they see a melodrama in which a mother opposes a young man's courtship of her daughter because the family fortunes may be saved by the marriage of the daughter to a wealthy, middle-aged, immoral businessman. Just as the businessman's mistress is about to entrap him and the young suitor is about to be arrested by the police, Embert reminds Evelyn that "this is about where we came in," and the couple leave the theater. In the novel which follows, Fuller narrated these same events, "not on the screen," but as they take place in the ordinary lives of Embert and Evelyn. Fuller gave the plot a happy ending in which true love defeats the scheming mother and the middle-aged suitor.

As a novel of social realism, Fuller's work has serious shortcomings. Despite his objection to the motion picture plot as melodramatic, Fuller's own work suffers from the same weakness, since the story develops out of incidents rather than from character. None of the characters comes alive; most of them, particularly the bond-salesman hero, Embert Howell, seem wooden figures which Fuller manipulated like the counters on a checkerboard. The strength of *Not on the Screen* lies in its general architectural outline, but Fuller's failure to work out the details in a credible manner almost overwhelms the excellence of his original design. This same weakness had been apparent earlier both in *The Last Rufuge* and *On the Stairs*.

Neither *Gardens of This World* nor *Not on the Screen* added greatly to Fuller's reputation, and very likely the same comment would have been valid for the novel which he left unfinished at his death. The fact, however, that Fuller, at seventy-two, after years of refusing to write novels, should have undertaken in rapid succession three novels seems evidence of a remarkable desire to strengthen his place in American letters.

CHAPTER 9

Behind Howells

On July 29, 1929, Hamlin Garland wrote in his diary:

Late at night word came of the passing of Henry Fuller. He carries with him a large part of my life for we have been intimate friends for more than a third of a century. Next to Howells he was my most trusted literary advisor. His judgment was so swift and so acute that I went to him in all matters where I felt at a loss. In a recent letter he said "I want to go down with all flags flying"—and he did. His amazing activity during the last year gave us all joy. . . . He was one of the quaintest, most elusive yet one of the most loyal of all our list of intimates. Wise, witty, subject to moods of depression and distaste for society—even for that of his friends, he was a joy to us all. His merry laugh was evidence of his essential joyousness of temperament and yet he could be most perverse and difficult. He will soon be a legend in Chicago.

I   A Contemporary Estimate

Although during the next few years Garland was to write a great deal about Fuller in *Roadside Meetings, Companions on the Trail, My Friendly Contemporaries,* and *Afternoon Neighbors,* he never added significantly to the comments which he made in his diary the night of Fuller's death. The image of Fuller which Garland's remarks expressed represented Fuller as his best friends knew him; and the impressive tributes which Anna Morgan collected in the succeeding months, though adding detail and illustration, only served to emphasize the soundness of Garland's estimate.

Long and close as their association had been since they met in 1894, Garland knew that there were areas in Fuller's life and personality which neither he nor any of Fuller's friends had ever penetrated. What Garland called "perverse" and "elusive" in Fuller referred not merely to his external peculiarities, many of which resulted from his bachelor ways of living, but to a certain inner reserve, a hard barrier which Fuller always interposed between his friends, including Garland, and himself.

As a result of this barrier, Garland's knowledge of Fuller was strangly limited. In estimating Fuller, Garland, like many others, was handicapped by his lack of knowledge about Fuller's boyhood, his family relationships, his financial resources, or the reasons for his partial participation in life. Fuller's contemporaries, especially Garland, probably never completely understood that side of Fuller which responded to "art," to the cultivation of one's own esthetic sensibilities, to the appeal of the expatriate life in Italy, to the artistry of Henry James, or to the fine points of literary style. Certainly, to the extent that Fuller was a romantic esthete whose bias favored Europe over America, Garland could neither share nor comprehend his friend's attitude.

II   The Dilemma of the Man

By the time Fuller completed high school, the traits of his personality that primarily shaped his career as a writer had already formed and hardened. Born into a family of Chicago's "old settlers" whose fortunes were declining, Fuller became, as a boy and as a young man, a diffident, sensitive, idealistic, self-effacing "loner." Nothing in his personality seemed likely to fit smoothly into the highly competitive, gregarious, and, often, not very ethical business life of the booming metropolis of Chicago. Thrust into this atmosphere to work as a clerk in a crockery store, Fuller rapidly developed a settled aversion to the marketplace and to what he believed to be the primitive idols that were worshipped there by the "cliff-dwellers."

Partly from a natural inclination, partly as an escape from an environment he already thought hostile, and partly as an area in which he could excel, Fuller concentrated his energies first upon academic achievements and then upon the acquisition of culture. His goal was to make himself no less than a master of prose style and an expert in architecture, the classics, music, and foreign languages. Of course, the more he lost himself in the pursuit of culture, the less suited he was to participate in the life of Chicago and the more he desired to examine for himself the focal point of his studies—Europe—Italy.

In many respects, Fuller's grand tour of Europe in 1879-80 must be considered the most important year of his life. It helped to solidify the pattern that his life was already assuming and gave him the impetus for writing. In addition, the trip meant for Fuller an escape from provinciality and a tremendous widening of his intellectual and emotional horizons. Most important of all, it dramatized the difference between the Chicago Fuller had begun to hate and the Europe he had dreamed about for years. When Fuller returned, the two poles of his life had been identified, established, and anchored; and he had had the experience that for the remainder of his life he ardently wished to recapture.

In the 1880's, Fuller first began to realize the implications of the dilemma being forced upon him. The difference which he noted between Howells and James offered a remarkable parallel to his own predicament; in fact, in the analogy he drew between them lay the core of his own dilemma. Fuller could grasp the logic and the soundness of Howells' position with regard to the use of American subjects and the involvement of the American writer in issues American; but Fuller knew himself ill-suited by temperament to participate in subjects and issues Chicagoan, while at the same time he was aware that his experience abroad had confirmed his attachment to Italy.

Valuable as the analogy with Howells and James was to Fuller in the 1880's, with a better vantage point he might have learned even more from Howells' experience considered by itself. As Fuller partly understood, Howells, about twenty years earlier, had had his European experience; but afterwards, Howells had been able to marry, cross over from Europe—cross over permanently—and accept a responsible position in the profession of letters. But, and Fuller may have sensed the difference though he failed to mention it, Howells had returned to a Cambridge, whereas Fuller had had to go back to a Chicago. In Cambridge, Howells had found a semblance of an intellectual tradition and could admire its leaders, Longfellow, Holmes, Lowell, and Norton, even while he moved ideologically farther and farther from their position. The bleakness of Chicago, the complete absence of a cultural tradition, and the lack of any place for the artist in the scheme of things, as well as its wrong-headed objectives for human striving almost overwhelmed Fuller. Howells, by contrast, had been able to involve himself in American issues and thereby to identify himself with the goals of the society of which he was a part.

For Fuller, however, the European experience had been too influential, his ties too close to the America of the "old settlers," and his literary allegiance to the Genteel Tradition of Lowell and Norton too strong for him to follow long in the footsteps of Howells. Not until the last decade of Fuller's life would he be able to approach the acceptance of modern America that Howells had already made before Fuller even began to write.

III   Fuller's Great Decade

Out of the tension produced by the contrast between his memory of Europe and the reality of Chicago, Fuller wrote *The Chevalier of Pensieri-Vani*. In Cambridge, both Lowell and Norton praised his achievement and spread the news about the discovery of a new talent in American letters. That Fuller's book of idealistic travel fiction was almost as much about Chicago as Italy, neither Norton nor Lowell fully comprehended. When Fuller restated his case in *The Chatelaine of La Trinité*, he made his critical attitude toward Chicago even plainer; but both books received praise for their charm, for Fuller's exquisite style, and for his romantic subject matter. Although they had a limited appeal, the audience was a select and vocal one. In the newspapers, literary journalists expressed their astonishment that such artistic and charming books as these could be written in Chicago; and Chicagoans, eager to boast about their city, adopted him as proof that Chicago had culture as well as hogs and could now compete on even terms with the East.

The line of cleavage between Fuller's first two books dealing with Italy and his direct examination of Chicago in *The Cliff-Dwellers* and *With the Procession* is not nearly so sharp as the change in subject matter would make it appear. Chicago had been an ever-present, if not always visible, force in both of the Italian volumes. The difference lay primarily in Fuller's shift from a romantic—he considered it Jamesian—approach to the realistic frontal assault of Howells. In *The Cliff-Dwellers*, he deliberately dropped the allegorical technique and spoke to the

matter directly and bluntly. In *With the Procession,* he produced a more artistic, less melodramatic, and, perhaps, less forceful evaluation; and, although Fuller was still not exactly in
accord with Howells' literary theories, his second Chicago book
was closer to Howells' practice than his first had been.

The shift in subject matter from Italy to Chicago, from the
Roman past to the American present, from the far away to the
familiar, required an equally pronounced change in literary
styles. Happily for Fuller, he had based his theory of the "style
absolute" primarily upon the necessity of an author's accom-
modating his manner of writing—the observance of the "fundamental proprieties"—to the literature he was creating. Accord-
ingly, Fuller sought to change his style from an instrument
suitable for rendering the charm of the Italian countryside and
the glories of the Roman past to a vehicle equally appropriate
for conveying the business and social competitions of modern
Chicago. The proof of his success in the observance of the fundamental proprieties in both styles lies in the fact that Charles
Eliot Norton and James Russell Lowell, spokesmen for the
Genteel Tradition, praised his Italian pieces as works of genuine
artistic beauty while such men as Theodore Dreiser, Floyd
Dell, and Sherwood Anderson acknowledged his Chicago volumes as forerunners of American naturalism.

Although Fuller continued to write throughout the 1890's,
he never again achieved the level of excellence that he attained
in *The Chevalier of Pensieri-Vani, The Chatelaine of La Trinité,
The Cliff-Dwellers,* and *With the Procession.* As the decade
closed, he made another effort to turn a disappointing visit to
Europe into a novel, but the book, whose title, *The Last Refuge,*
implied his attitude toward Europe, proved a failure. Thus, as
the century ended, Fuller felt he had lost in Europe and lost
in America. His great decade ended upon a gloomy note.

IV   The Last Years

In the years that followed, Fuller wrote less and less, and
what he did write received little praise. Of all his production
after 1900, only the satires in *Under the Skylights* add significantly to his permanent reputation. *Lines Long and Short, On
the Stairs,* and *Bertram Cope's Year* must be considered experi-

ments that fall far short of Fuller's best work. In the final decade of his life, however, Fuller resolved, to a considerable degree, the dilemma of his life. He freed himself from the desire to escape to Europe, and his last journey abroad in 1924 convinced him, as never before, that he belonged in America. Fuller had finally crossed over permanently; and like Howells many years earlier, Fuller found a place for himself in the profession of letters. As a free-lance writer on general literary subjects, he effectively used his vast knowledge of the arts to express a conservative literary point of view. With this acceptance of a place within literary affairs, he managed to come to terms with Chicago itself.

His last two novels, *Gardens of This World* and *Not on the Screen,* although in many respects unsatisfactory as novels, may be viewed indirectly as Fuller's statement of his final position on the matter of Europe and Chicago. In the first, although Americans are still trying to plunder its treasures, Europe has become chiefly a place for the "gardens of this world" where those who wish may find occasional peace and quiet away from the ugliness of contemporary life. For Fuller, Europe no longer represented the temptation to live in the past or to ignore the issues of the present. The change in his attitude toward Chicago may be inferred from *Not on the Screen.* As a young writer, he would have been profoundly disturbed by the dullness and lack of direction which he observed in the lives of young stock salesmen like Embert Howell; but, in 1929, Fuller found in one of America's dull young men an appropriate subject for his fiction. William Dean Howells would have approved the change in Fuller.

Only a few weeks before Fuller's death, Hamlin Garland had predicted that Fuller would rank next to Howells. In his reply, Fuller indicated the point at which he had finally arrived. "Yes, I'll fall in somewhere behind . . . Howells, and be glad to. He'll come out all right, and so shall I. In twenty years or less the U.S. will be indisputably the one great country of the world, and in twenty years more Chicago will be the biggest town in it and the central city of the well-known globe. *Then* everything will fall into place, H.B.F. included, and the place will be plenty good enough" (June 10, 1929).

V Fuller's Place

Fuller's modest wish to fall in somewhere behind Howells has proved, in the main, an accurate forecast of his place in American literature. By bracketing him with Stephen Crane, and by crediting him with leading the movement of realism in American literature, Theodore Dreiser probably overstated Fuller's achievement;[1] nevertheless, as Howells himself recognized, when Fuller wrote *The Cliff-Dwellers* and *With the Procession,* no other novelist had rendered so accurately as Fuller the everyday life of the middle-class citizen in the booming metropolises of America. As an early and skillful practitioner of the technique of realism, as an accomplished satirist, and as a literary craftsman and stylist, Fuller has a very respectable place in the history of American letters.

In addition to an historical importance, the humanistic critic of the twentieth century must also acknowledge Fuller's permanent place among those writers who at their best have courageously protested against the forces in American democracy which operate to force the individual into a constricting social conformity, who have advanced the cause of art and beauty in American life, and who have in their own lives dramatized the need for spiritual values amidst an increasingly materialistic society.

Notes and References

To conserve space, as many references as possible have been placed in the text. Except in the instance of *The Chevalier of Pensieri-Vani,* where the edition published in 1892 by the Century Company has been used, quotations from Fuller's novels have been made from the first edition cited fully in the bibliography. Because the repositories for manuscript material, except in certain instances, are not included in the notes, the following sources should be understood: for Hamlin Garland's diaries, the Huntington Library; for Fuller's letters to Garland, the University of Southern California Library; for Fuller's letters to Howells, the Houghton Library of Harvard University; and for all other unpublished material, the Newberry Library.

Chapter One

1. Quoted in *Tributes to Henry B.,* ed. Anna Morgan ([Chicago] 1929), p. 19.
2. *Ibid.,* pp. 19, 27.
3. "A. C. A.," MS, Newberry Library; quotations from Fuller's account of his life at the Allison are from this manuscript.
4. As in the case of Frank Donaldson, Flora Van Nostrand became a character in "Edmund Dalrymple," where her failure to arouse Dalrymple's interest in her causes her "a vague sense of insufficiency and disappointment." Dalrymple, whose character appears based upon Fuller himself, seems "to regard her as a mere person, a generalized human creature with no definite place on either side of that incisive line which divides the race into its two elemental sections."
5. "A Legacy to Posterity," MS, Newberry Library.
6. *Ibid.*
7. *Cf. On the Stairs,* p. 27.
8. "A Legacy to Posterity."
9. *Ibid.*
10. *Ibid.*
11. Diary begun August 25, 1876, MS, Newberry Library.

Chapter Two

1. "A Legacy to Posterity," August 1 [1877].
2. Diary begun August 25, 1876.
3. "A Year in Europe," MS journal, Newberry Library, August

30, 1879; all subsequent quotations in this chapter have been taken from this source; the dates of Fuller's entries are indicated in the text.

4. On April 4, 1880, he made the same point: "At the Academy I dutifully saw the great Titians, Vernoneses and Carpaccios which everybody sees; but I shall not claim to have looked at them at all understandably or appreciatively. . . ."

5. On April 13, 1880, Fuller described his visit to the house of the Capulets and the tomb of Juliet; years later, when he was writing *The Chatelaine of La Trinité,* he made extensive use of this material in chapter eight.

Chapter Three

1. "Pensieri Privati," MS, Newberry Library; *cf.* Constance Griffin, *Henry Blake Fuller* (Philadelphia, Pa., 1939), p. 8.

2. *Ibid.*

3. MS, Newberry Library. All that survives of Fuller's journal of his second tour of Europe which lasted six months is this thirty-two page manuscript. That Fuller wrote nothing about his travels after he reached Rome seems most unlikely.

4. *Life,* III (January 24, 1884), 47-49; III (January 31, 1884), 62-63.

5. *Life,* III (March 27, 1884), 173.

6. *Life III* (April 3, 1884), 187-89; III (April 10, 1884), 201-3.

7. *Life,* III (June 26, 1884), 355-57.

8. Chicago *Evening Post,* February 7, 1903, p. 4.

9. Chicago *Tribune,* October 4, 1884, p. 16.

10. "Pasquale's Picture," *The Current,* IV (July 11, 1885), 27-28; Fuller reprinted the story in *From the Other Side,* pp. 205-29.

11. Fuller's essay has been edited by Darrel Abel in *Modern Fiction,* III (Summer, 1957), 159-64; quotations from the essay are taken from this text.

12. *The Century Magazine,* XXV (November, 1882), 28.

13. "Two Notable Novels," *The Century Magazine,* XXVIII (August, 1884), 632-33.

14. *Cf.* Henry James, *Hawthorne* (New York, 1879), pp. 41-43.

15. Fuller to Minna Smith, May 24, 1891, Newberry Library.

16. *Ibid.*

17. *Ibid.*

18. H[arriet] M[onroe], "Henry B. Fuller," *Poetry: A Magazine of Verse,* XXX (October, 1929), 34.

19. Fuller's memorandum-book was sold along with the manuscript of *The Chevalier of Pensieri-Vani* and other items from his estate; the catalogue of the Chicago Book and Art Auctions, Inc., describing the manuscript, contains Fuller's descriptions of his work.

Chapter Four

1. Chicago *Herald,* February 28, 1892.
2. Chicago *Evening Post,* August 28, 1895, p. 1.
3. Newspaper clipping, Newberry Library.
4. Boston *Gazette,* September 13, 1891. The article began with the statement: "Good things are continually coming out of Nazareth." Papers from other cities joined in the attack on Chicago. The Louisville *Courier-Journal* (April 30, 1892), for example, found it "quite impossible to conceive of such a story as the one in question being written by a person who has any affinity or any dealings, however remote, with Chicago."
5. Agnes Repplier, "A By-Way in Fiction," *Lippincott's Monthly Magazine,* XLVII (June, 1891), 760.
6. Newspaper clipping, Newberry Library.
7. See Chapter II, p. 31.
8. Later in the book, Fuller again facetiously referred to the demands he made upon the reader. "It may be that some of you have resented my disposition to assume your familiarity with the obscure and inaccessible relics of mid-Etruria, and perhaps I was wrong in expecting even a remote acquaintance with matters so difficult and recondite. I hope I shall not repeat the error if I take for granted a certain familiarity with the outlying hills of Rome, which, however much indeed neglected, are sufficiently interesting and sufficiently accessible to receive the amount of attention that is justly their due" (70). Although Fuller's remarks were made with tongue-in-cheek, the fact remains that the great majority of place names in *The Chevalier of Pensieri-Vani* are wholly unfamiliar to anyone but a person thoroughly conversant with the small towns of Italy. The strange place names, as Fuller intended, add to the atmosphere of erudition and romantic charm that pervades the book.
9. Earlier the Prorege had illustrated his concept of national government in terms of a building, while Occident had chosen as his figure a river (102-3).
10. "My Early Books," unpublished MS, quoted by Griffin, *Henry Blake Fuller,* p. 33.
11. Although Edwards (1859-1950) was at the beginning of a distinguished career as an illustrator and a painter of portraits and murals, shortly after *The Chatelaine of La Trinité* was published, the drawings were sharply criticized. The reviewer for *The Harvard Monthly* (December, 1892) remarked that "the illustrations are the worst things in the book: they are about as bad as pictures can be. Many of them are of the size and shape of 'kodaks,' and seem to be the work of a very inexperienced photographer. The one on page

24 [34], representing the Duchess's carriage, is especially vile, though some of the other pictures, of a different shape and size, are very little better. The decorations detract seriously from the interest of the text" (p. 130).

12. See Chapter II, pp. 43-44.

Chapter Five

1. "Westminster Abbey," *The Century Magazine*, XLV (March, 1893), 700-18; "Holy Week in Seville," *The Contributor's Magazine*, I (April 22, 1893), 2-7.

2. Chicago *Morning News Record*, September 14, 1892, p. 4.

3. *Ibid.*

4. *Ibid.*, September 16, 1892, p. 4.

5. *Ibid.*, September 14, 1892, p. 4.

6. *Ibid.*

7. Carl W. Condit, *The Chicago School of Architecture* (Chicago and London, 1964), p. 44.

8. *Atlantic Monthly*, LXXX (October, 1897), 541.

9. *The Chatelaine of La Trinité*, pp. 64-66.

10. MS notebook, Newberry Library.

11. *Ibid.*

12. *Cf.* Griffin, *Henry B. Fuller*, pp. 40-41.

13. See Chapter IV, pp. 77-78.

14. *The Chatelaine of La Trinité*, p. 62.

Chapter Six

1. *Harper's Bazaar*, XXVI (October 28, 1893), 883; Howells intended the review for *Harper's Weekly*.

2. Mildred Howells, ed., *Life in Letters of William Dean Howells* (2 vols.; New York, 1928), II, 39.

3. Fuller to Howells, November 3, 1893.

4. William Dean Howells, "Life and Letters," *Harper's Weekly*, XXXIX (June 1, 1895), 508.

5. *Ibid.*; see also William Dean Howells, *Heroines of Fiction* (2 vols.; New York and London, 1903), II, 246-253.

6. Howells, "Life and Letters," p. 508.

7. "*The Cliff-Dwellers*," p. 883.

8. "The Great American Novel," *American Spectator*, I (December, 1932), 1. Dreiser's essay is reprinted in *The American Spectator Year Book*, ed. George Jean Nathan and others (New York, 1934), pp. 16-25. See also Dreiser's introduction to Frank Norris' *McTeague* (Garden City, N.Y., 1928), p. viii; and *Letters of Theodore Dreiser*, ed. Robert H. Elias (3 vols.; Philadelphia, Pa., 1959), II, 612.

9. "Half a Dozen Story-Books," *Atlantic Monthly,* LXXVI (October, 1895), 556.

10. "Chicago Letter," *The Critic,* XXVI (May 18, 1895), 371.

11. "With the Procession," *The Chap-Book,* III (June 1, 1895), 72.

12. James Huneker, "Raconteur," *Musical Courier, XXX* (June 19, 1895), 18.

13. *Ibid.*

14. "Life and Letters," p. 508.

15. Sara Norton and M. A. DeWolfe Howe, eds., *Letters of Charles Eliot Norton* (2 vols.; Boston and New York, 1913), II, 217.

16. *Ibid.,* II, 225.

17. Fuller to Hamlin Garland, June 7, 1895.

Chapter Seven

1. "The Upward Movement," p. 534.

2. Harriet Monroe, *A Poet's Life* (New York, 1938), p. 132.

3. *Letters of Charles Eliot Norton,* II, 218.

4. "The Upward Movement," p. 534.

5. Anna Morgan, *My Chicago* (Chicago, 1918), p. 188.

6 For Garland's account, see *Companions on the Trail* (New York, 1931), pp. 370-72.

7. Fuller, "Notes on Lorado Taft," *The Century Magazine,* LIV (October, 1908, 618; cf. Fuller, "Taft's 'Solitude of the Soul,'" Chicago *Post,* April 20, 1901, p. 6; and Hamlin Garland, *Roadside Meetings* (New York, 1931), pp. 264-65.

8. *Ibid.,* p. 267.

9. "The Upward Movement," p. 534.

10. Fuller, "Chicago's Book of Days," *The Outlook,* LXIX (October 5, 1901), 291.

11. Fuller to Garland, January 27, 1894.

12. Fuller to Paine, October 10 [1895], Huntington Library.

13. *The Chap-Book,* IV (December 1, 1895), 71-80.

14. Fuller's play was published in Griffin's *Henry Blake Fuller,* pp. 77-86.

15. Fuller, quoted by Mary J. Reid, "Henry B. Fuller," *The Book Buyer, XII* (January, 1896), 822.

16. "Editorial," *Elite,* May 23, 1896.

17. "Mr. Fuller in a New Field," *The Critic,* XXVIII (May 16, 1896), 349.

18. "Editorial," *Elite,* May 23, 1896.

19. Josephine Huneker, ed., *Intimate Letters of James Gibbons Huneker* (New York, 1924), p. 23.

20. "Mr. Fuller's 'Puppet-Booth,'" *The Critic,* XXIX (September 12, 1896), 156.

21. "Mr. Fuller in a New Field," *The Critic,* XXVIII (May 16, 1896), 349.

22. Fuller to Garland, March 2, 1897.

23. Fuller to Garland, January 15, 1897.

24. January 21, 1897, Newberry Library.

25. On April 5, 1898, Miss Morgan presented the play in her studio, and on April 9, Fuller lectured on Goldoni at Miss Morgan's studio. Garland noted in his diary: "It was capital talk—just like Fuller witty, full of odd turns of thought and above all unconventional. We all snickered disgracefully at his odd witticisms. He read from notes which he rolled up into wads and threw away." See also Garland, *Roadside Meetings,* pp. 272-73.

26. See above, Chapter IV, p. 71, and note 8.

27. *The New Flag Satires* ([Chicago] 1899). Quotations from Fuller's pamphlet have been published by Robert Morss Lovett, "Fuller of Chicago," *The New Republic,* LX (August 21, 1929), 16-18.

Chapter Eight

1. Garland, *Roadside Meetings,* p. 274.

2. Fuller's editorials include "Why Is the Anglo-Saxon Disliked?" January 6; "The Modern Man and Nature," January 20; "How to Make Good Aldermen," April 14; "A National Park at Lake Itasca," April 21; and "When in Doubt—Send Flowers," August 11.

3. The articles appeared, respectively, May 17, 1902; June 14, 1902; November 8, 1902; and February 7, 1903.

4. *Cf.* Griffin, *Henry Blake Fuller,* p. 63.

5. Fuller's clippings, Newberry Library.

6. "Henry B. Fuller," p. 39; see also *A Poet's Life,* p. 286; and Morgan (ed.), *Tributes to Henry B.,* p. 31.

7. Respectively, Chap. IX, Vol. IV, *The Industrial State, 1870-1893,* edited by Ernest Ludlow Bogart and Charles Manfred Thompson; and Chap. II, Vol. V, *The Modern Commonwealth, 1893-1918,* edited by Ernest Ludlow Bogart and John Mabry Matthews (Springfield, Illinois, 1920).

8. *Cf.* Susan J. Turner, *A History of The Freeman* (New York and London, 1963), pp. 112-15.

9. Garland's Diary, June 28, 1924; in successive revisions to his diaries, Garland added emphasis to the passages referring to Fuller's disappointment over the trip with Shepherd; and in *Afternoon Neighbors* (New York, 1934), pp. 182-83, Garland phrased the matter very bluntly.

10. *Cf. Afternoon Neighbors,* pp. 130, 339.

Chapter Nine

1. *Letters of Theodore Dreiser,* ed. Elias, I, 185; Dreiser included Brand Whitlock with Crane and Fuller. See also Chap. VI, p. 109, n. 8.

Selected Bibliography

PRIMARY SOURCES

A Note on Manuscript Sources and Bibliography
The Henry B. Fuller Collection of the Newberry Library is the largest single repository of Fuller manuscripts. Additional manuscript material of primary importance has been assembled by the library of the University of Southern California, the Henry E. Huntington Library, the Houghton Library of Harvard University, and the library of the Chicago Historical Society.

The following bibliography of Fuller's writings and secondary materials about him represents a selection of the most important items. For a descriptive bibliography of Fuller's books, see Jacob Blanck (comp.), *Bibliography of American Literature* (New Haven, Connecticut, 1959), III, 257-61; and Bradford Fuller Swan, *A Bibliography of Henry Blake Fuller* (New Haven, Connecticut, 1930); for virtually complete listings of Fuller's writings consult the bibliographies in the dissertations by Bernard R. Bowron and Paul Rosenblatt listed below.

1. BOOKS

The Chevalier of Pensieri-Vani together with Frequent References to the Prorege of Arcopia. By Stanton Page [pseud.]. Boston: J. G. Cupples Co., Publishers [1890].

Ernest Ludlow Bogart and John Marby Mathews. Springfield,
The Chevalier of Pensieri-Vani. New York: The Century Co., 1892.
The Chatelaine of La Trinité. New York: The Century Co., 1892.
The Cliff-Dwellers: A Novel. New York: Harper and Brothers Publishers, 1893.
With the Procession: A Novel. New York: Harper and Brothers Publishers, 1895.
With the Procession: A Novel. Introduction by Mark Harris. Chicago: University of Chicago Press [1965].
The Puppet-Booth: Twelve Plays. New York: The Century Co., 1896.
From the Other Side: Stories of Transatlantic Travel. Boston and New York: Houghton Mifflin and Company, 1898.
The New Flag: Satires [Chicago, 1899].
The Last Refuge: A Sicilian Romance. Boston and New York: Houghton Mifflin and Company, 1900.
Under the Skylights. New York: D. Appleton and Company, 1901.

Selected Bibliography

Waldo Trench and Others: Stories of Americans in Italy. New York: Charles Scribner's Sons, 1908.

Lines Long and Short: Biographical Sketches in Various Rhythms. Boston and New York: Houghton Mifflin Company, 1917.

On the Stairs. Boston and New York: Houghton Mifflin Company, 1918.

Bertram Cope's Year: A Novel. Chicago: Ralph Fletcher Seymour, 1919.

Gardens of This World. New York: Alfred A. Knopf, 1929.

Not on the Screen. New York: Alfred A. Knopf, 1930.

2. IMPORTANT UNCOLLECTED WRITINGS

"Americanization of Europe's Youth." New York *Times Magazine,* January 25, 1925, p. 15.

"Art in America." *The Bookman,* X (November, 1899), 218-24.

"Chicago." *The Century Magazine,* LXXXIV (May, 1912), 25-33.

"Chicago's Book of Days." *The Outlook, LXIX* (October 5, 1901), 288-99.

"Development of Arts and Letters." *Centennial History of Illinois.* Vol. IV. *The Industrial State, 1870-1893.* Ed. Ernest Ludlow Bogart and Charles Manfred Thompson. Springfield, Illinois: The Illinois Centennial Commission, 1920.

'The Duchess Visits Her Home Town." *The Bookman,* LX (December, 1924), 413-16.

"Errol's Voice." *The Century Magazine,* CVIII (August, 1924), 527-35.

"The Growth of Education, Art and Letters." *Centennial History of Illinois.* Vol. V. *The Modern Commonwealth, 1893-1918.* Ed. Ernest Ludlow Bogart and John Mabry Mathews. Springfield, Illinois: The Illinois Centennial Commission, 1920.

"Howells or James?" Ed. Darrel Abel. *Modern Fiction,* III (Summer, 1957), 159-64.

"Holy Week in Seville." *The Contributor's Magazine,* I (April 22, 1893), 2-7.

"An Industrial Utopia." *Harper's Weekly,* LI (October 12, 1907), 1482-83.

"Is Great Literature of the Future to Come from American Continent?" Chicago *Evening Post,* June 14, 1902, p. 9.

"Italian Fiction." *The Critic,* XXX (May 29, 1897), 365-66.

"The Life-Tale of Pearl McRoy." *Everybody's Magazine,* XXIII (September, 1910), 380-89.

"The Long and the Short of It." *Life,* III (June 26, 1884), 355-57.

"The Melting Pot Begins to Smell." New York *Times Book Review,* December 21, 1924, p. 2.

"Miranda Harlowe's Mortgage." *Atlantic Monthly,* LXXXVI (November, 1900) , 671-75.

"Mural Paintings at the Fair, First Paper." Chicago *Record,* May 25, 1893.

"A New Field for Free Verse." *The Dial,* LXI (December 14, 1916), 515-17.

"New Forms of Short Fiction." *The Dial,* LXII (March 8, 1917), 167-69.

"Notes on Lorado Taft." *The Century Magazine,* LIV (October, 1908), 618-19.

"O That Way Madness Lies." *The Chap-Book,* IV (December 1, 1895), 71-80.

"A Plea for Shorter Novels." *The Dial, LXIII* (August 30, 1917), 139-41.

"Quartette." *Harper's Monthly, CXXI* (November, 1910), 934-38.

"The Romance of a Middle-Aged Merchant and His Female Private Secretary." Chicago *Tribune,* October 4, 1884, p. 16.

"Silence." *Scribner's Magazine,* XLVIII (October, 1910), 430-31.

"The Story of Naphtha." *Life,* III (April 3, 1884), 187-89; III (April 10, 1884), 201-3.

"Striking an Average." *The Saturday Evening Post,* CLXXIII (May 25, 1901), 3-5, 14-15.

"Taft's 'Solitude of the Soul.' " Chicago *Post,* April 20, 1901, p. 6.

"The Thirteenth Goddess." *Harper's Monthly,* CXLVIII (December, 1923), 125-27.

"A Transcontinental Episode." *Life,* III (January 24, 1884), 47-49; III (January 31, 1884), 62-63.

"Under the Crest of Shishaldin." *Everybody's Magazine,* XVI (June, 1907), 809-15.

"The Upward Movement in Chicago." *Atlantic Monthly,* LXXX (October, 1897) , 534-47.

"Westminster Abbey." *The Century Magazine,* XLV (March, 1893), 700-18.

"World's Fair Architecture." Chicago *News Record,* September 14, 1892, p. 4; "Second Paper," September 16, 1892, p. 4.

SECONDARY SOURCES

1. DOCTORAL DISSERTATIONS

BOWRON, BERNARD R. "Henry B. Fuller: A Critical Study." Unpublished Ph.D. dissertation, Harvard University, 1948. A sympathetic, generally reliable study with an excellent bibliography.

JACKSON, KENNY. "An Evolution of the New Chicago from the Old: A Study of Henry Blake Fuller's Chicago Novels." Unpublished

Ph.D. dissertation, University of Pennsylvania, 1961. An able critique of Fuller's relationship to Chicago.

PEARCE, RICHARD A. "Chicago in the Fiction of the 1890's as Illustrated in the Novels of Henry B. Fuller and Robert Herrick." Unpublished Ph.D. dissertation, Columbia University, 1963. A balanced survey of the work of Fuller and Robert Herrick of interest to all students of the Chicago group of writers.

ROSENBLATT, PAUL. "The Image of Civilization in the Novels of Henry Blake Fuller." Unpublished Ph.D. dissertation, Columbia University, 1960. Fuller's work deals with two types of societies, the civilized and the barbaric, represented by Europe and Chicago. The bibliography of Fuller's writings, arranged chronologically, is especially helpful.

2. BOOKS AND ARTICLES IN PERIODICALS

BROOKS, VAN WYCK. *The Dream of Arcadia: American Writers and Artists in Italy 1760-1915.* New York: E. P. Dutton and Co., 1958. In a chapter devoted to Fuller, Brooks provides a brief survey of Fuller's Italian stories.

CONDIT, CARL W. *The Chicago School of Architecture.* Chicago and London: The University of Chicago Press, 1964. An excellent commentary on architectural trends with many illustrations of the "cliff-dwellings" of Chicago.

DELL, FLOYD. "Chicago in Fiction," *The Bookman,* XXXVIII (November, 1913), 270-77; Part II, XXXVIII (December, 1913), 375-79. In a comprehensive survey of the leading novelists of the "Chicago School," Dell characterizes Fuller as a gentle satirist.

DREISER, THEODORE. "The Great American Novel." *The American Spectator Year Book.* Ed. George Jean Nathan. New York: Frederick A. Stokes and Co., 1934. Contains Dreiser's praise of Fuller as a leader of realism.

DUFFEY, BERNARD. *The Chicago Renaissance in American Letters: A Critical History.* [East Lansing, Michigan] The Michigan State University Press, 1956. In an interesting chapter on Fuller's career, Duffey concludes that the difficulty which prevented Fuller from writing major literature was personal rather than stylistic.

ELIAS, ROBERT H. (ed.). *Letters of Theodore Dreiser.* 3 vols.; Philadelphia, Pa.: University of Pennsylvania Press, 1959. In several letters, Dreiser refers to Fuller as the leader of American realism and acknowledges his influence upon Chicago writers.

[Farrar, John] "The Literary Spotlight," *The Bookman,* LVIII (February, 1924), 645-49. In this sketch, written after Fuller began to achieve a reputation as a critic and a reviewer, the writer con-

cedes Fuller the sensibility and intelligence to write masterpieces but finds him lacking the necessary vitality.

GARLAND, HAMLIN. *Afternoon Neighbors*. New York: The Macmillan
Company, 1934. Next to the diaries upon which they are based,
Garland's series of autobiographical volumes provide the most
comprehensive source of information about Fuller's life and
artistic interests.

———. *Back-Trailers from the Middle Border*. New York: The Macmillan Company, 1928.

———. *Companions on the Trail*. New York: The Macmillan Company, 1931.

———. *A Daughter of the Middle Border*. New York: The Macmillan
Company, 1921.

———. *My Friendly Contemporaries*. New York: The Macmillan
Company, 1932.

———. *Roadside Meetings*. New York: The Macmillan Company,
1931.

GELFANT, BLANCHE HOUSMAN. *The American City Novel*. Norman,
Oklahoma: University of Oklahoma Press, 1954. Discusses Fuller
in relation to other Chicago novelists, particularly Dreiser.

GRIFFIN, CONSTANCE M. *Henry Blake Fuller: A Critical Biography*.
Philadelphia: University of Pennsylvania Press, 1939. A brief
biographical essay valuable for the use of manuscript material
and as the only previously published volume about Fuller.

HARRIS, MARK. "Fuller and the American Procession." Introduction.
With the Procession by Henry Blake Fuller. Chicago and London:
The University of Chicago Press [1965]. Interesting comments by
a contemporary writer in the latest reprint of a novel by Fuller.

HOWELLS, Mildred (ed.). *Life in Letters of William Dean Howells*. 2
vols.; New York: Doubleday, Doran and Company, Inc., 1928.
Howells' letters to Fuller are important for an understanding
of Fuller's attitude toward his work.

HUNEKER, JAMES. "The Seven Arts. Mr. Fuller's Masterpiece," *Puck*,
LXXVIII (September 11, 1915), 10, 21. An early expression of
Huneker's admiration for Fuller.

HUNEKER, JOSEPHINE (ed.). *Intimate Letters of James Gibbons
Huneker*, New York: Boni and Liveright, 1924. Several letters
acknowledge Fuller's influence upon Huneker.

LAWRENCE, ELWOOD P. "Fuller of Chicago: A Study in Frustration,"
American Quarterly, VI (Summer, 1954), 137-46. An important
review of Fuller's contribution in which the writer emphasizes
Fuller's sense of frustration as the source of his failure to fulfill
his early promise.

LOVETT, ROBERT MORSS. "Fuller of Chicago," *The New Republic*, LX

(August 21, 1929), 16-18. While recognizing Fuller's talent, Lovett blames the decline in Fuller's work after 1900 on his resentment over American conduct in the Philippines.

[Monroe, Harriet] "Henry B. Fuller," *Poetry*, XXXV (October, 1929), 34-41. A valuable estimate of Fuller's strengths and weaknesses by a friend who knew him for most of his life.

MONROE, HARRIET. *A Poet's Life: Seventy Years in a Changing World*. New York: The Macmillan Company, 1938. Supplies information about Fuller's connection with *Poetry* and about members of the Little Room.

MORGAN, ANNA (ed.). *Tributes to Henry B.* [Chicago] Ralph Fletcher Seymour Publisher, 1929. The more than seventy tributes and evaluations of Fuller in this volume constitute one of the most important published sources of information about the man and his circle of friends.

NORTON, SARA, and M. A. DeWOLFE HOWE (eds.). *Letters of Charles Eliot Norton*. 2 vols.; Boston and New York: Houghton Mifflin Company, 1913. Norton's letters to Fuller at the beginning of his literary career reveal his affinity with the older New England writers.

MURRAY, DONALD M. "Henry B. Fuller, Friend of Howells," *South Atlantic Quarterly*, LII (1953), 431-44. Offers a thoughtful comparison between Fuller and Howells emphasizing Fuller's withdrawal from American life in contrast to Howells' eager participation.

OPPENHEIM, J. H. "Autopsy on Chicago," *The American Mercury*, XL (April, 1937), 454-61. Attributes the highbrow reputation of the Chicago *Evening Post* to the literary standards established by Fuller but asserts that his example was "anything but wholesome" for Chicago.

PEATTIE, DONALD CULROSS. "Henry Blake Fuller," *Reading and Collecting*, II (January, 1938), 19-20. Reminiscences and anecdotes, not always flattering, of Fuller's later years.

PIERCE, BESSIE LOUISE. *A History of Chicago*. Vol. III. *The Rise of a Modern City 1871-1893*. New York: Alfred A. Knopf, 1957. The most comprehensive and scholarly of the histories of Chicago, indispensable for an understanding of Fuller's life and work.

POLLARD, PERCIVAL. *Their Day in Court*. New York and Washington: The Neale Publishing Company, 1909. Includes a brief but valuable discussion of Chicago literary figures.

REPPLIER, AGNES. "A By-Way in Fiction," *Lippincott's Monthly Magazine*, XLVII (June, 1891), 760-65. Early in Fuller's career, Miss Repplier's appreciation of *The Chevalier of Pensieri-Vani* helped to establish his reputation; later this sketch was reprinted in her *Essays in Miniature*.

Shultz, Victor. "Henry Blake Fuller: Civilized Chicagoan," *The Bookman*, LXX (September, 1929), 34-38. Writing shortly after Fuller's death, Shultz examines Fuller's entire career and stresses the praise of his writing from Norton, Lowell, Repplier, Howells, Huneker, Dreiser, Wilder, and Van Vechten.

Seymour, Ralph Fletcher. *Some Went This Way*. Chicago: Ralph Fletcher Seymour Publisher, 1945. Easily one of the best of the volumes of memoirs dealing with Chicago and Chicago artists.

Turner, Susan, J. *A History of The Freeman*. New York and London: Columbia University Press, 1963. An analysis of Fuller's reviews and contributions to *The Freeman*.

Van Vechten, Carl. *Excavations: A Book of Advocates*. New York: Alfred A. Knopf, 1926. In a chapter devoted to Fuller, Van Vechten praises Fuller's Italian work but argues, unconvincingly, that had Fuller become an expatriate in Italy he would have developed his talent to a greater degree than he did.

Index

DATE DUE